Praise for S̶a̶

Becoming Your Best Self

"Intuition is our most natural way of knowing. This book helps you return to innate clarity and flow with easy, common-sense tips and insights. It guides you into your truest self and life."—Penney Peirce, author of *Frequency* and *The Intuitive Way*

"This is the one book about intuition that is so practical, grounded, accessible, and exceptional that even the most skeptical reader can't help but take it to heart."—Raphael Cushnir, author of *The One Thing Holding You Back: Unleashing the Power of Emotional Connection*

"A wise and loyal companion for traversing the turns, twists, and precipices on the path of intuitive development. Sara Wiseman has been aptly named, for she not only leads you to a higher place of knowing, but to a stronger place of being."—Debra Lynne Katz, author of *You Are Psychic, Extraordinary Psychic,* and *Freeing the Genie Within*

"A clear, thorough, and eminently useful guide to all things sixth-sensory related, this book will help you activate, hone, and increase your psychic abilities in no time flat. It's the book the intuitive world has been waiting for. I love it!"—Tess Whitehurst, author of *The Good Energy Book* and *Magical Housekeeping*

"Wiseman's work helps elevate us to our uppermost level, where we can propel ourselves to our own highest level without judgment and grief."—Jodi Livon, author of *The Happy Medium*

"Written with humor, wisdom, and clarity, Sara Wiseman's book will help anyone who wants to understand the psychic or angelic experiences they've had, or to learn how to connect directly to the Divine. Highly recommended."—Miriam Knight, founder of *New Consciousness Review*

"Frank, funny, and infinitely kind, Sara helps readers recognize and interact with the sixth sense through simple exercises that gently open the 'mind's ear.'"—Carol Kline, author of *Streetwise Spirituality*

"A masterful guide to awaken the unquestioning truth inside us all. Anyone who adores inner exploration will devour this book and relish the freedom to know and trust themselves in unimaginable ways."—Erin Donley, New Renaissance Bookshop

"With her well-honed wit and nail-on-the-head advice, Wiseman tells it like it is—and in her endearing and bell-ringing way, leads you deeper until you find your inner self."—Vicky Thompson, editor of *New Connexion Journal*

"Developing our intuitive potential is essential with the shift in our collective awareness. Sara Wiseman's much-needed book is an excellent resource for safely expanding these capacities."—Susan Wisehart, holistic psychotherapist and author of *Soul Visioning*

Your Psychic Child

"Hands-down, this book is a responsible and positive approach to what can often be a scary subject for parents and children alike. *Your Psychic Child* might also be called a manual for reaching the Divine." —Meg Blackburn Losey, PhD, author of the internationally best-selling *The Children of Now*

"Sara Wiseman helps us learn to honor kids' wisdom and keep it alive so our young people can grow to be fully integrated human beings, inspired creators, and well-rounded leaders."—Penney Peirce, author of *Frequency* and *The Intuitive Way*

"Sara Wiseman writes with extraordinary wisdom, clarity, and humor about how to recognize your sensitive children's special gifts, and how to help them avoid the pitfalls while developing their skills. She offers great insights on both parenting and developing intuition that would benefit any reader. Warmly recommended."—Miriam Knight, founder of *New Consciousness Review*

"A must-have guide for helping children to hone their intuitive gifts and parents to become the conscious creators they long to be."—Vicky Thompson, author of *Life-Changing Affirmations* and editor of *New Connexion Journal*

"Sara Wiseman is the Erma Bombeck of the psychic crowd . . . I recommend *Your Psychic Child*, not only to parents and the general public, but also to our children themselves. Kids could and should read this book, too."—P. M. H. Atwater, author of *Beyond the Indigo Children*

"This book will open the hearts and minds of parents whose children are trying to find their way through a maze of confusion caused by their gift of knowing, feeling, and seeing what others cannot."—Shirley Enebrad, independent TV producer and author of *Over the Rainbow Bridge*

Writing the Divine

"The lessons are reasonable, creative, and full of both insight and guidance. This is a good one."—Anna Jedrziewski, *New Age Retailer*

"Sassy and approachable, *Writing the Divine* is a great read filled with practical information on how to listen for the messages from the Divine. But take it seriously. There is wisdom in this work. *Highly recommended*."—Sophy Burnham, author of the *New York Times* bestselling *A Book of Angels*

"Wiseman lovingly shares with us the treasures of divine guidance entrusted her by spirit, while gracefully offering us wisdom culled from her own experience. Wiseman shines in teaching us the true purpose of life: our soul growth."—Michael J Tamura, visionary teacher, spiritual healing pioneer, and award-winning author of *You Are the Answer*

"Wiseman demystifies the channeling process, making a sacred act simple. With wit and delightful humor, she shares practical tools for connecting with the divine inner voice."—Vicky Thompson, editor of *New Connexion Journal* and author of *Life-Changing Affirmations*

Becoming
Your
Best Self

About the Author

Sara Wiseman experienced a spiritual awakening in 2004 when she unexpectedly received Divine teachings from a spirit guide. Four years later, she received *The 33 Lessons*, an intensive experience of channeled writing that begins, "The purpose of life is soul growth," and is part of her first book. Sara is the author of *Writing the Divine: How to Use Channeling for Soul Growth & Healing* and *Your Psychic Child: How to Raise Intuitive & Spiritually Gifted Kids of All Ages*. She hosts "Ask Sara" on Contact Talk Radio, writes regularly for *Retailing Insight* and other national New Age publications, is a contributor to DailyOm, and has released four healing CDs with her band Martyrs of Sound. She works privately with clients worldwide.

For more information, please visit www.sarawiseman.com.

Becoming
Your
Best Self

The Guide to Clarity, Inspiration and Joy

Sara
Wiseman

Llewellyn Publications
Woodbury, Minnesota

Becoming Your Best Self: The Guide to Clarity, Inspiration and Joy © 2012 by Sara Wiseman. All rights reserved. No part of this book may be used or reproduced in any manner whatsoever, including Internet usage, without written permission from Llewellyn Publications, except in the case of brief quotations embodied in critical articles and reviews.

FIRST EDITION
First Printing, 2012

Cover background image: iStockphoto.com/Goldmund Lukic
Cover design by Adrienne Zimiga

Llewellyn Publications is a registered trademark of Llewellyn Worldwide Ltd.

Library of Congress Cataloging-in-Publication Data
Wiseman, Sara, 1962–
   Becoming your best self : the guide to clarity, inspiration and joy / Sara Wiseman. — 1st ed.
      p.   cm.
   Includes bibliographical references.
   ISBN 978-0-7387-2794-3
   1. Self-actualization (Psychology)—Miscellanea. 2. Intuition—Miscellanea. 3. Spiritual life—Miscellanea. I. Title.
   BF1999.W638 2012
   131—dc23
                                        2012004567

Llewellyn Worldwide Ltd. does not participate in, endorse, or have any authority or responsibility concerning private business transactions between our authors and the public.
   All mail addressed to the author is forwarded but the publisher cannot, unless specifically instructed by the author, give out an address or phone number.
   Any Internet references contained in this work are current at publication time, but the publisher cannot guarantee that a specific location will continue to be maintained. Please refer to the publisher's website for links to authors' websites and other sources.

Llewellyn Publications
A Division of Llewellyn Worldwide Ltd.
2143 Wooddale Drive
Woodbury, MN 55125-2989
www.llewellyn.com

Printed in the United States of America

Other Books by Sara Wiseman

Writing the Divine: How to Use Channeling for Soul Growth & Healing

Your Psychic Child: How to Raise Intuitive &
Spiritually Gifted Kids of All Ages

Dedication

For all of you . . . Divine beings in Earth bodies, sublime souls who have stepped onto this unmarked path and walked with me a while . . . this book is yours.

Acknowledgments

I am grateful for the support of Dr. Steve Koc, Krista Goering, Jason Carter, Raphael Cushnir, Erin Donley, Margie Gibson, Debra Lynne Katz, Miriam Knight, Jodi Livon, Andrea Mathews, Penney Peirce, Silver Sorenson, Vicky Thompson, Leslie Venti, Rev. Drew Vogt, Tess Whitehurst, the amazing folks at Llewellyn, New Renaissance Books, East West Bookshop, Contact Talk Radio, Satiama, and DailyOm, and my children.

When you exist in highest vibration, all things are possible.
Thus all information, all layers of Universal dimension,
are available to you in instantaneous movement of mind.

—The Messages

Contents

Preface

This is a book of secrets, widely known but little told. It is a tale of the Universe, written in the song of trees, the wisdom of mountains, the rush and whisper of ocean and sky, the immutable magic of the galaxies that contain us. It is also a story writ in the human heart, with all its pain and beauty, longing and passion.

In short, this is no ordinary book.

Within these pages, you'll learn how to open your innate intuitive skills in an extraordinary way—in full connection to the Divine/One/ All that both surrounds us and is us. By learning how to become One with everything, you'll easily be able to see, hear, sense, understand, and heal in ways you've never before thought possible.

And while this book may seem simple upon first reading, rest assured—it is not. The information presented here is serious work, and if you dedicate yourself to fully engaging with these exercises, and to walking the mystic, magical path of intuitive awakening, you will emerge from this journey transformed.

This is not a book for the faint of heart, the sly, the power hungry, or for any who prefer to stay asleep in this lifetime.

It is for those who are ready to awaken.

It is for those who seek healing.

It is for those in need of grace.

As we enter a time of yet another great shift for humanity, the answers you seek are readily available to you. It is simply a matter of knowing how to listen, how to see and feel. With each step you take upon the intuitive path, Universal guidance becomes clear.

Introduction

Intuition speaks through the voice of the Universe:
it is a quiet whisper at some moments, a loud shout at others.
There is no time this voice is not present.

—The Messages

What if you could open to Divine guidance, simply by asking?
What if you could "read" signs and symbols from the Universe?
What if you understood your highest possibility for this lifetime?
What if you could communicate with Divine beings at any time?
What if you could heal the present, past, and future?
What if you could live in Universal flow?

The truth is you can, simply by using your intuition—a natural-born ability that's innately yours—even if you've never used it before, or even realized you had it.

Some believe that intuition is a gift that belongs to only a chosen few—an ancient secret closely guarded by a handful of gurus, a smattering of mystics, a legion of psychics armed with crystal balls and 1-800 numbers.

Yet this is not so.

Intuition just is—a sixth sense that's as natural or normal to us as hearing or seeing or any of the other senses. What's more, there's no time you're without it—intuitive information is always switched on, like a cosmic GPS ready to provide clear direction as you navigate your life's path.

At its essence, intuition is the ability to wake up to the Universe and to claim your birthright as a Divine being in an earth body. It's an opening, an awakening, a hero's quest—and when you're ready for it, it's ready for you.

Waking from the dream

It all sounds so easy, doesn't it—this idea of waking up. All you gotta do is open your eyes, swig a cuppa joe, and you're there, right? And yet so many of us remain fast asleep for years, decades—sometimes our whole lives.

I can say this, because I spent most of my adult life sleeping. In fact, every time that annoying Universal alarm clock started to buzz and blare with wakeup calls throughout my twenties, thirties, and into my forties, I'd hit that snooze button as fast as possible!

In fact, I'd still be asleep today—if the Divine hadn't decided to bring out the big guns and do a cosmic intervention.

Which it did.

My first uh-oh-this-is-getting-serious wakeup call was a near-death experience (NDE) in 2000—no gentle nudge on the shoulder, that! Except it didn't work. While NDEs do the trick for most folks—the majority of people who see the white tunnel report having instant life transformations—well, I guess I was a stubborn case.

Oh sure, I did see God at the time of the NDE; I had the whole luminous, radiant experience. But instead of this transforming my life, it created chaos. And instead of heading into bliss and happiness and joy, like most everybody else who's had NDEs, I headed a different direction.

Down.

In a few short years following my NDE, I had post-traumatic stress disorder.

My dad died.

I got divorced.

I lost my business.

Sigh.

And yet, even with this nonstop deluge of Divine wakeup calls, I still fought to stay asleep, grabbing those covers and pulling 'em over my head!

That's when the Universe finally decided to get serious. Really serious. It was time for them to send somebody from "up there" down here, to wake me up in person.

Now, I must qualify what comes next by saying I never expected to meet a spirit guide. That's because at the time I didn't believe in them.

Spirit guides? Angels? Entities?

Seriously?

You gotta be kidding.

Thus, when that first spirit guide floated across my living room floor in 2004, with a density of being not quite human but decidedly more dense than air, a visible entity who had something to say to me—and in fact, wanted me to write it down—well, let's just say I woke up pretty darn fast.

I woke up.

I believed.

And I was terrified.

As I sat there trembling with my laptop on my lap, the aforementioned spirit guide, Hajam, a short guru wearing drapey clothing and with a tendency to burst into giggling or dancing at any given moment, began talking to me—and I realized my life as I'd known it was about to change.

I took "dictation" from this spirit guide, my own personal Mr. Wakeup from the Universe, for several months—and each time that I received his messages via channeled writing, I found that my ability to "hear" was getting stronger. In fact, so was everything else energetic in my life—I was shifting and sliding from low vibration to high, moving and turning and spinning between confusion and awareness as my consciousness began to expand.

As it turns out, Hajam was not the only spirit guide I would meet in this lifetime. It was as if the opening of my "window" to one Divine messenger made it possible for others to also come through.

Which they did.

Four years later, in 2008, I received 120 pages of channeled writing called *The 33 Lessons*, an intensive experience of channeling from three guides: Constance, Miriam, and Archangel Gabriel, who arrived in my dining room as I sat and scribed for hours. It was during the receiving of these messages, which are part of my first book, *Writing the Divine*, that I finally, really, and completely woke up.

I became conscious of myself as One.

With every hour that I sat in *direct connection* to the Divine, channeling these extraordinary messages, I was infused with the energy of the Universe. And after a certain amount of infusion—one day, one month, four months—after a certain point, something cracked open.

Mostly, it was my heart.

And with the opening of my heart, everything began to change.

Intuition as spiritual path

The spiritual path and the psychic path are one and the same. Thus, if you do spiritual practice of any kind for long enough, eventually you will become psychic. Conversely, if you work in the psychic realm long enough, eventually you'll have a spiritual opening.

They are the same paths, taken from different starting points.

Soon after I channeled *The 33 Lessons*, astonishing psychic abilities began to surge forth in my being. I began to know things. I began to see things, I began to understand how to make life decisions clearly and easily, without doubt or fear. I understood that all is energy, and that by following energy, we can begin to live in Universal flow.

These abilities opened incrementally, staring in 2008. First, I opened as a channel. Soon after, I became clairvoyant, experienced medical intuition, suddenly understood how to work with energies and how to work beyond time and space, and finally, I opened to mediumship—the ability to connect with the departed.

Even now, my abilities continue to expand.

I don't say this as some kind of laundry list of "look what I can do."

That's not it at all.

This is not a tale of one person.

It is your story as well.

Every single human being on this earth has the ability to become intuitive—to wake up from the earth dream, and to enter the new reality of the Divine. Each of us is destined for a spiritual awakening, in which we become aware of a whole new paradigm: the experience of living as a Divine being living with an earth heart.

This was true for me.

It is also true for you.

Integrating after awakening

The trouble was, even though I could suddenly do all this psychic stuff, I wasn't sure how I was doing it. How did it all work? What were the steps? I looked for books to explain it, but what I found did not reflect my experience. I found plenty of "woo woo," and a whole lot of old superstitions. But most of what I found didn't fit my particular paradigm.

It's said that when the student is ready for the teacher, the teacher will appear.

Yet in my case, I began to have a sneaking suspicion that once again, the Universe had a few more tricks up its sleeve for me.

There would be no master teacher for me.

In fact, to my shock, I began to realize that I was supposed to be the teacher.

How was I supposed to do that? Be the teacher, when I didn't even know how I did what I did? Run the class, when I didn't even know the curriculum?

And yet this was my calling.

Thus with this task in front of me, I set about figuring out how it all worked. Because one thing I knew for sure was this: if I could delve deep and explore and understand how all this worked from my own experience, I could surely teach this to you.

My source for these teachings comes from my spirit guides, who've led, directed, taught, and helped me experience firsthand all that I needed to know—these Divine lessons will never be finished! I've had lovely breakthroughs with colleagues, especially Rev. Drew Vogt and Debra Lynne Katz. And of course, I've also learned immeasurably from the thousands of beautiful souls I've walked with, as they journey along this path that is both psychic and Divine.

I am honored to accompany you, as you embark on your own journey.

A word about *The Messages*

Scattered throughout this book you'll find *The Messages*, spiritual teachings I've received in channeled writing. These particular messages were provided to me by two tall, pale guides, Ragnar and Ashkar, who began to appear to me in early 2009. They are elongated, luminous beings who often appear as a twinned entity, and they have provided me with extraordinary teachings about energy, metaphysics, intuition, time, space, vibration, and healing. If you would like read more of these and other messages as I receive them, visit www.sarawiseman.com.

Audio help for the journey

In this book I've provided exercises that contain complete, step-by-step instructions on how to do intuitive work on your own; you may also choose to work in tandem with a partner or group. Both methods work beautifully!

However, I've had so many requests for guided meditations that I've created downloadable audio courses to assist you in your work. You'll find everything you need at www.sarawiseman.com.

Part One

Opening

one

Awakening

At your core you are intuitive—this is your natural state of being.
There is no separation between your Divine self and your earth self.
—The Messages

Learning to use your intuitive abilities isn't to be taken lightly—it's a serious skill that can bring you serious benefits. Why? Because when you understand how to access Divine information in all the layers and levels of the Universe, then everything becomes lucid.

That means that instead of floundering about wondering what job offer to accept, what life path to follow, what partner to marry, what city to live in, or if you really should get that adorable Great Dane puppy even though you are living in a three-hundred-square-foot studio in New York City—everything all becomes suddenly, reassuringly clear.

Intuition isn't only about seeing the future. It's about understanding where you are now, and what your highest possibility or next best step is from this point forward. It's about working with Universal energy—a.k.a. the Universe/Divine/God/One/All—and learning how to "see," "hear," or "know" what your highest path is, where you will grow the

most as a person, and how you will experience the most soul growth
in this lifetime. It's about working beyond the boundaries of time and
space, to heal relationships, situations, and your own human heart.

Rest assured, the Universe/Divine/God/One/All or whatever name
you have for the infinite ineffable is more than happy to provide you
with guidance, every time you ask. And when you do learn how to ask
for, receive, and trust this guidance—well, your life begins to move in
Divine flow, and then, frankly, everything shifts:

- Instead of floundering, you flower.
- Instead of questioning, you create.
- Instead of worrying, you live in wonder.
- Instead of being fearful, you live in trust.

Ready for the fast lane?

For example, imagine that you have an older car. You've had it for a long
time, and it's served you well. "Old Betty" gets decent mileage, her loan
is paid off, she's easy to drive and reasonably safe. The trouble is, the old
gal isn't feeling well—she belches smoke, leaks oil, and can't be trusted
for horsepower. Sure, you can take her to the grocery store, but aside
from that, she's too worn out for much.

Now, imagine one day you and Old Betty drive past a new car lot.
And there on the lot, sparkling like a diamond in the sun, is a whole
new kind of car. It's hybrid, electric, eco. It's low-mileage, high-safety,
and it's got cup holders and flower holders and seat warmers. It's got
Internet and Nav—the works! But best of all . . . are you ready for this?
This car can take you anywhere. Not just to work or for grocery runs.
Not just on road trips. But all the way into the past! All the way into the
future! All the way everywhere in the Universe, through all layers and
levels of time and space!

Wanna trade in?

Of course, you can always keep "Old Betty," and let her ferry you to
work and back at maximum granny speed, sputtering smoke and Cas-
trol. Or, you could branch out and try a *whole new kind* of vehicle—one

that expands the possibilities in your life by a million, billion, gazillion fold!

The moral of this story isn't about driving in the fast lane or even about making the necessary shift from an oil-based economy. Instead, it's this: like this amazing new car, intuition is an amazing new way to use your brain, and it can take you anywhere. Yet so many of us are still clunking around in our old beaters.

Why is this?

It's true that as humans we utilize so little of our brainpower that we've gotten used to a lower level of performance. Yet we don't have to live this way. We can choose to expand our awareness, and to dip into a cosmic consciousness that's unlimited, exponentially useful, enlightening, and miraculous. And all of this can happen instantaneously, from the first moment we understand that at our core, at our very essence, we are intuitive beings.

The information you receive from the cosmos is collective consciousness, available to all at any time. This information is available to you, instantaneously and without ceasing, from the moment you begin to listen.
—The Messages

Trust is the key

If you've read this far, I can safely assume you've decided to trade in "Old Betty" and switch to a whole new method of mental transportation. So, strap on your seat belt, and let's talk about what it takes to be intuitive: what it looks like, feels like, and what might surprise you along the way.

That said, what you'll need to learn first are the "secrets" surrounding intuition, most importantly that:

• You can trust that intuition arrives from Divine source.

• You can trust intuition to lead you toward your highest possibility.

• You can trust that intuitive information is accurate and true.

Out of everything in this book, trust is the most important lesson you'll need to learn. It's also the hardest.

When I teach intuition workshops, one of the first things I'll do to work through the "trust" issue is to take folks into some easy exercises in which we'll receive information about their life's path and purpose.

What usually happens goes something like this—we'll do the exercise, people will receive intuitive information, and at the first question break, hands will shoot up and everyone will clamor, "But how do I know it's *true?*" Common variations of this question include "How do I know it's not my imagination?" or "How do I know I'm not making things up?" or "How do I know it's not my thoughts?"

You get the idea.

At this point in the workshop, I don't even bother to answer. I merely suggest that folks be patient, bear with me, hang on for a minute, hold their horses—because clarity is coming. Next, we return to our exercise and go a little deeper this time, and when the second question break comes around, there are no longer any questions.

This is because whether you trust your intuitive experience—either right from the start or a little bit later—eventually, the profundity of the experience will overwhelm you.

At some point in the process, you will surrender your disbelief.

You will trust that what you are receiving is real, true, and Divine.

And at the exact, instantaneous moment that this happens, you will discover that everything in your life has begun to change. The energy of intuition is Divine, and when you activate, awaken, or open to it, everything surrounding you becomes infused with this magical, mystical energy.

Getting started

Ready to start? Fantastic. We're going to take it step by step, slow and easy, so you have time to process as you go. First things first, we'll start every exercise in this book with the same *setup* or preparation. Doing things the same way every time will help you move more quickly into the layer or level you'll need to do this work.

As part of your setup before you start an exercise, you'll want to:

- Read the complete exercise. Because you'll have your eyes closed as you work, you won't be able to refer to the instructions as you go. No worries! Simply read through and then trust that you'll remember what you need.

- Stay in connection. If you should forget what you're supposed to do or get distracted in the middle of an exercise, don't open your eyes or break concentration. Just let your experience take you where it will.

- If you're working with a partner or a group, have one person read the exercise aloud, while the others do the exercise. This is a lovely way to experience this work.

Next, to do your setup, please:

- Find a quiet spot, such as a room where you can shut the door and be alone.
- TOYC (turn off your cellphone!)
- Sit easily in a chair or on a sofa with your feet on the floor and your hands at your sides or in your lap. Close your eyes. If you have physical issues, adjust as you need to so that you are comfortable.
- Take a deep breath in through your nose, out through your mouth. Repeat two to twelve times, or until you begin to feel a slight shimmering or tingling in your brain or on the top of your head. This is both from the oxygenation caused by deep breathing, and also because you are already beginning to transition to the sublime layer or level where intuitive information resides.

Ready? Here we go!

Exercise: Entering the Vision

1. Do your setup as described on the previous page.
2. Now, imagine that your body is staying here in the chair, but your spirit is detaching from your body, like Peter Pan's shadow

did from Peter Pan. This can look like whatever you want. Your spirit might be golden, or luminous, or it might be misty and shadowy—it's not important what it looks like. Simply notice it.

3. Allow your spirit to find a small crack in the window or door of the room, and let it escape out of that space. Allow your attention to go with it. Soon, you'll be able to see or imagine yourself looking down on yourself: in the room, or perhaps you'll see or imagine yourself outside your room, looking down out your roof, or perhaps you'll find or imagine yourself all the way out in space, looking down at Planet Earth.

4. You'll notice I say "see" or "find" or "imagine," as if they are all one term. At this point, for our purposes, they are. If you can't yet trust that you are "seeing" something intuitively, then allow yourself to "see" it by imagining it. At this point, for our first exercise, it makes absolutely no difference how this happens. We're getting warmed up. We're activating a new ability. At this point, how you get there doesn't matter one whit! Do whatever works—any way you can "see" or "imagine" or "visualize" is just fine.

5. Now, direct your spirit to view a vision, image, or situation. *This vision will answer a question.* How can you answer a question when you don't even know what it is? Well, that's how intuition works! During this first experience, you may move slowly, tentatively, not sure what's happening. But as you work through this book, you will find that it becomes faster and easier to do intuitive work. Eventually, it will become as automatic for you as breathing.

6. As your spirit moves around to show you the answer to this question, notice what happens: do you see yourself moving, flying, going into another space? Do you see something familiar, or is it new? Are there people you know in this vision? Are there objects? Is there a symbol or archetype? Watch this scene or image display itself, without any expectation. Now, you might not only be "seeing" at this point. Some people might find they "hear" a

word or words in what I call their "mind's ear." Some people also "see" words as images, in their head. Some people feel emotions, or have memories suddenly emerge, or feel things in their body. Simply notice, and let what happens happen.

7. Stay in this realm of exploration until you feel it is complete. Now, gently count yourself out (or have your partner or group leader do this), counting aloud from ten to one, directing yourself to be fully present in the room, with eyes open, when you return.

Before you think or talk about your experience, or do anything else at all, please write your answers to the questions below. Even if you're not sure what you experienced, write whatever comes into your mind.

1. What was the vision or message you received? Describe it in detail. If you are not sure what you saw, simply write down anything that comes to mind at this time.

2. What surprised you about this vision or message? Write down anything that comes to mind.

3. What emotions, memories, or revelations did you have when you received this vision or message?

4. How did you feel at the start of this exercise? How did you feel when it was complete?

Please turn to page 241, where you will find the question that you answered in this first exercise.

To see, to hear in other dimensions is not difficult;
in one breath, you are there.
In one breath, you become One.

—The Messages

---

two

Asking

In asking, the window is opened; all you need to know
blows in upon a Divine wind.
—The Messages

We're only at chapter 2, and yet some of you have already experienced an *A-ha!* moment while completing the previous exercise! As you're starting to see, intuition works fast—and once you get the hang of it, you'll be able to work instantaneously, at any time.

Of course, others of you are more at a place of "Huh?" than "A-ha!" right now. This is fine! Rest assured that even if you don't think you're "getting it," energy is moving, intuition is opening—you're on the path, even if it doesn't seem like you've taken many steps forward.

So, what happened when you saw your vision? What were you thinking about, and what came into your mind? When I've used this exercise in workshops, it's fascinating to hear what people come up with even before I've revealed the question. For example:

"I saw myself driving up to a huge stop sign, and I knew that I was supposed to stop," an older man shares.

"I saw a wedding ceremony, and I 'floated' down into the celebration. A man walked up to me in a tuxedo, and I saw it was my neighbor Dan. He was the groom, and he asked me where his bride was," a woman discloses.

When workshop participants share, it's sometimes a little uncomfortable at first—most folks are hesitant to reveal their innermost thoughts to people they've just met. Often, they preface their remarks with "It doesn't make any sense, but . . ." or "I'm sure I'm making all this up, but . . ."

Imagine then, when I reveal the question that they've just answered intuitively! There are gasps, cheers, and laughter as everyone has a collective *A-ha!* moment for what their own intuitive visioning revealed. At that point, I remind them that they answered this question before they knew what the question was.

To recap, the question was:

What is the relationship or situation that requires my attention most right now? What is the soul lesson I'm being asked to pay attention to surrounding this relationship or situation?

As we go around the room and share, it becomes clear how light and bright the energy in the room has become—almost as if a Divine floodlight has suddenly switched on high. The air is tingling with energy. Everyone's pretty blown away by how exactly their vision answered the question:

"I'm supposed to retire this year," the man who saw the stop sign announces to the group, and a look of relief floods his face. "I knew that already, but now I really know."

"I think I'm in love," the woman who saw the wedding ceremony whispers, and then breaks down into tears. "I can't even talk right now."

What intuition reveals

Often, intuition tells us *what we already know*. This includes:

- What's ahead in the future
- What's deep in the past

- What we feel in our hearts, and

- What our highest possibility or next best step is for happiness, expansion, and *soul growth*

For example, the man who saw the stop sign? As he shared more with the group, we learned that while he craves ending his thirty-eight-year career, he's put off retiring.

"I'm only sixty-two. Officially, I'm supposed to wait another three years," he explained as the group listened sympathetically. "But I feel in my heart that it's time to move on." Seeing the information intuitively in a "blind" reading, he suddenly understood that, official years left or not, it was time for him to go.

As for the woman who'd visualized her groom? Hesitatingly at first, then passionately, she told the group that she'd loved her next-door neighbor for years, but had never had the courage to tell him. "At my age," she shared, "it just felt silly." But after her "blind" reading, she said, she was determined to wait no longer.

Two days later, she emailed me to say that she'd marched across the street to his house and invited her fifty-nine-year-old self in for coffee. Four months later, they were married.

When we use intuition to reveal our heart's true longing, we are always moving towards our highest possibility. This level of knowing is always Divine.

The information you receive from the Universe is collective consciousness, available to all at any time.
This information is available to you,
instantaneously and without ceasing,
from the moment you begin to listen.

—The Messages

Where does intuition come from?

There are so many theories on how intuitive abilities work. Cynics chalk it up to "coincidence" or "luck" or even "smoke and mirrors." Fair enough. If you're cynic or a left-brained thinker used to figuring everything out with rational analysis, then it's going to be quite a paradigm shift for you to accept intuition.

In the past, psychiatrists such as Carl Jung held that intuition was merely our subconscious mind at work. Recent research has posited that intuition is simply the right brain hard at work. Or, even a kind of "super sensitivity"—like über detectives, psychics are able to "read" the subtle clues presented by a person's voice, appearance, even handwriting, and make logical (and often correct) guesses from there.

Religious folks posit that intuition is the voice of God—in Quaker and other practices around the world, for example, intuition is recognized as "the still, small voice" that is revealed in prayer.

Spiritualists, mediums, and channels say they access information from other realms. Others in the holistic or New Age fields dub the source of intuitive information as collective soul, cosmic voice, unified field, Akashic records, and so on.

In other words, there's a whole lotta belief systems out there, all trying to explain how it is that we *can* know what we *don't* know.

And I say—all of 'em are right.

What you believe affects your experience

If you want to receive intuitive information, you can. And the wrappings or belief system that you hold around where the information comes from doesn't make much difference. In my experience of working with folks who are all over the map in terms of their religions, cultures, backgrounds, education, ages, and more, I've found that:

- It's most likely that intuition will arrive to you in the guise of the belief system you prefer to follow, and

- While the vocabulary may be different, the source is always the same: Divine/One/All/Universe—the ineffable idea that we and the Universe are One.

- All intuitive information is instantaneous, or outside of time; in other words, you know before you "know."

- All intuitive information has emotional content, or a deeper meaning behind the obvious.

- Anyone can receive intuitive information, as long as they ask.

Asking is key

Say you're an eight-year-old kid, and you really, really want to go to Mr. Cutter's Candy Store. Now, your mom's not that excited about candy, and your dentist is even less so. But you're eight! What do you care about cavities? Besides, it's a fantastic candy store, brimming with gobstoppers and chocolate drops and horehounds and salt-water taffy and lemon drops and caramel clusters and gigantic swirling lollipops in every color of the rainbow.

Awesome.

Except . . . you're eight. You're too young to walk there by yourself. You're too young to drive yourself there. You gotta ask to be taken.

Now, there are several very effective eight-year-old methods of doing this . . .

- The incessant whine. "Can we go to the candy store? Can we? Can we?" Repeat every three minutes for one hour. This method is extremely annoying—and extremely effective.

- The guilt game. "Everyone else in third grade gets to go to Mr. Cutter's Candy Store, so why not me?"

- Begging. "Oh, pulleeeeeeeeeeeeeeese! I'll do anything, anything, anything!"

- Saintly behavior. "Mom, I made my bed, did my homework, fed the dog . . . Can I give you a back rub? You sure look pretty today . . ."

You'll have reasonable responses with the above approaches; put in enough effort, and they'll probably work. However, your mom won't be super happy with you. She knows a sneak/cheat/liar/manipulator when she sees one!

No, a much better method would be just to ask. To just say, "Hey, Mom, I'd really like you to take me to Mr. Cutter's Candy Store. I'm only eight, and I can't walk there by myself, and I can't drive myself, and I was hoping you could take me."

Trust me: the direct approach works like a charm.

And, as luck would have it, the same goes for intuition.

Ask, and you'll receive

There's a whole lot of whoo-ha associated with psychic abilities. Sometimes, we think that being able to access intuitive information will in some ways make us different, better, or happier. Well, let's put it this way: it won't . . . but it will.

In my own experience, having an intuitive awakening did not:

- Add bazillions of dollars into my bank account
- Skyrocket me to the top of the *New York Times* bestseller list
- Buy me a Maserati
- Help me drop twenty pounds
- Cure my obsession with silly comedies
- And so on

I'm basically still me—older and more patient, to be sure. I've definitely got some brand-spanking-new brain skills—and I'm here to help you develop your own. But that core person who has always been "me," the particular Earth being who's living this particular Earth life this time around? Well, that person's still here.

However . . . even though a lot of the surface things in my life haven't changed, I have been transformed by this journey. Once you step off the edge of "normal life" and begin to rub shoulders with angels and spirit guides, begin to transverse the layers and levels of other realms, begin to move in the different vibrational ranges of energy, and start to understand—not just intellectually but in your whole body, spirit, and soul—that we are indeed One: no separation, no membrane, no line, not one iota of difference between us, God, and the Universe . . . well, this understanding and experience changes you!

I have found that much of my old personality has dropped away.

Many of my old ego needs no longer exist.

Most of my fear has simply dissolved.

My heart is open, and opens more each day.

I understand that my purpose here on Earth is to write and teach and serve who shows up—and not to worry about exactly how that will happen.

That said, I'm very far from perfect. I certainly have my share of personal faults and failings—just ask my family and friends!

But through my work in intuition, and because I connect with the Divine for hours at a time as I do my work, I have shifted. I have changed. I have been transformed.

Understand this, as you take you own journey.

This will also happen to you.

Asking opens your windows

Most of the time, we humans keep our heads down. We do our jobs, take care of our families, run carpool, do errands, pay our bills, and so forth.

However, there is more.

Your guides, your angels, all of the other entities in other realms are standing around while you go about your daily tasks, just *waiting* for you to notice them. With any opening you give them, anything at all, they will attempt to provide you with useful information that will benefit and assist you in your life.

Say a prayer? They're there.

Meditate? The whole posse shows up.

Ask for assistance? A legion of angels arrives.

Request some help? It's a done deal.

The problem is . . . oh dear, and it's a doozy . . . most of the time, *we don't ask.* We walk around with our egos and our opinions and our facts, and we don't even know that this amazing help is available to us, at all times, in any situation, 24/7.

Sometimes we're scared to ask for help.

Sometimes we're too proud.

Sometimes we don't think anything can help us.

Sometimes we think that if we let our hearts crack open that tiny little bit to ask for assistance, help, or healing, we will shatter, explode, and be forever broken.

Or the pain will hurt so much that we won't be able to bear it.

But with the Divine, it doesn't work that way.

They (spirit guides angels, saints, Holy Ones, etc.) are here to help you. They're on your side. You don't have to be afraid.

If you can accept this idea—that all of those in the etheric realms are there to help you, not harm you—then you're ready to ask.

Exercise: Heart's Opening

This one's really short, and really sweet. And best of all, it works like a miracle. Or, in fact, it may be one. Don't ask me how, or why, or request mathematical equations to show you how it's calculated in quantum theory; I don't know that stuff. What I do know is this—miracles are common when you're working in the ethers. It's just how the Divine runs it.

1. First, start with your setup as you did on page 13. Within seconds, you will find yourself relaxing into a very light, effortless trance—the very slightest shift of consciousness.

2. Now, imagine that your heart is a beautifully wrapped box in your chest. Picture this in your mind or your "mind's eye." Don't worry if you can't actually "see" it; just imagine it, or think about it. It all works the same, energetically.

3. Using your imagination, pretend you are unwrapping that box, until you have uncovered all the many layers that have covered

your heart. Notice what the layers are like as you move them away. Take as long as you need.

4. Now, imagine that you have reached your spiritual heart, right there in your chest. And carefully, gently, with the utmost love, ask your heart to crack or "open" one tiny little sliver. During this process, your heart keeps functioning. Everything works beautifully. Your heart just opens, an infinitesimal degree.

5. Next, ask the Divine/Universe/God/All/One to receive. Just say, in your mind or aloud, "I am ready to receive intuitive information" or "I ask to receive Divine guidance," or however this phrase arrives to you in your mind. Repeat it like a prayer or chant if you like.

6. Notice the peace that has come over you, and the feeling of expansion in your heart.

7. When you are ready, count backward slowly from ten until you are back in Earth reality. Then, open your eyes and go about your day, remembering that your heart has been opened, and you have asked to receive.

8. Take a moment, and write or reflect on this question: What did you experience as your heart opened? Write about anything that came up, and explore this until you are done exploring.

What happens next? Oh, nothing more than miracles, healing, and transformation! All will arrive to you from the moment of your asking—as if a door that was once closed has just swung open wide and will never be closed again.

Over time, you will learn to keep your windows
open more often, or even most of the time.
Please, we ask that you keep opening your windows!
—The Messages

three

Receiving

*The moment you open your window, there is a shift in your perception.
There is a sense of expansion, of lightness on the skin, as you become aware
of Universal presence. This awareness is instantaneous.*

—The Messages

Wanna open your window? All you need to do is ask.

In fact, there's nothing else required. There's no need to change your behavior, habits, or lifestyle. No qualification test, no best practices, no joining fee. You don't need to attend an expensive psychic institute, or spend hours chanting mantra, or trek around India in nothing but a dhoti, or buy a special crystal pendant that someone claims will open your third eye.

I say this, because many spiritual seekers work very hard at getting their habits "clean" in terms of spiritual and physical practice. Now, it's certainly lovely for the body to meditate three hours a day or practice Bikram yoga. It's certainly fine to have clean physical habits in diet and nutrition—you'll likely feel a lot better and live a whole lot longer. But in terms of initially experiencing intuition, it doesn't really matter what your spiritual or physical practice is.

Not everyone agrees with me—already, I can hear psychic pundits exclaiming that you'll receive intuitive information much more clearly when you live clean . . . and this is true. However, living clean is not a *requirement* for an initial intuitive opening.

Divine intuition meets you wherever you are.

You also needn't be a nice person to open intuitively (although of course I hope you are!). You can be crazy messed-up, cranky, difficult to live with, and entangled in all kinds of trouble: business snafus, chaotic friendships, relationship dramas. You can be failing, unhappy, and ill. You can be mad at everyone, in complete denial of your own weaknesses, fully resistant to reasonable advice, arms folded against any kind of spiritual opening or awakening or religious practice . . . heck, you might not even believe in God/One/All/Universe.

Lucky for you—lucky for all of us—the Divine doesn't really care who or where you are when you start to open. In fact, sometimes life crises, really bad personal behavior, or "bottoming out" as they call it in A. A., are the first steps toward opening. Sometimes it takes a doozy of a wakeup call: a near-death experience, a serious illness, accident, divorce, bankruptcy, loss, grief—this might be what it takes to start opening you up.

It's nice if you've got some spiritual development under your belt, or you've been working on personal growth, or you've been actively processing your "stuff." It's helpful if you eat well and avoid toxic substances. It's a little easier if you've already started on your path and you've made it up a few foothills already.

But it's not required.

That's because intuition isn't some kind of exclusive club, where you have to know a special secret handshake to get in. It's accessible to all— you're already a member.

It all starts with asking

The only requirement to becoming intuitive is to ask. Which, if you completed the exercise in the last chapter, you already did.

"What?" you say, incredulously. "I've already turned the key? I've already flipped the 'on' switch? I've already said 'all systems go'?"

Yep.

It's that easy.

Once you've asked to receive intuitive information from the Divine, things start to move. That's because in the instant you ask—or even before that instant of asking—you effectively open your *windows*. What's a window? In simplest terms, I'd say it's a kind of portal or conduit or jump track between realms. When you open your window to the Divine, then "they" are able to communicate with you, and you're able to communicate with them.

We'll explore who "they" are in chapter 9, but for now, in simplest terms, "they" are the spirit guides, ascended masters, elevated beings, saints, and Holy Ones who most frequently communicate with us—the entities who provide us with intuitive information, help guide us in our life on this earth, show us the path of highest possibility, and help us move forward in our soul growth. These entities also have the ability to open their windows quite a bit bigger and wider and through more layers and levels than we can. That means they can communicate with us here in the earth realm, but they can also communicate with other beings in other realms, too. They have a much farther reach than we do—they can jump multiple layers and levels with ease.

Layers and levels

Layers, you say? Levels?

Well . . . to satisfy those of a scientific bent, I must admit that I don't actually know how the concept of etheric layers works. Do they work like a layered bean dip, with beans on the bottom, guacamole in the middle, cheese on top? Maybe. And what about levels—are these like levels in a building? Is there some cosmic elevator operator asking, "Going up? What floor?" Hmmmm.

Layers and levels are simply the terms that I choose to work with. They were first given to me in channeled writing, and now I find they're remarkably simple to work with. I understand them, and most folks I work with understand them, too.

Of course, other much more complex theories abound: quantum physics, string theory, the many musings of metaphysics, the origins of the Universe promoted by different scientists, pundits, religions, cultures, groups. The brain boils, the intellect intellectualizes, the head spins—so many theories!

However, regardless of what the "truth" actually is—or even if there is such a thing—what I've found, and what you will discover also, is that working with the idea of layers and levels makes it easy for our brains to understand how to enter in to a place where we can communicate with the Divine. It's a tool that our brain can use—no PhD in quantum physics required.

And while I don't have a scientific definition of layer or level, I would argue that we don't always have to know how something works in order to use it. Columbus might not have understood everything about the ocean, but he did understand how to harness wind and waves, and in that way sail to the New World. You probably don't know how your computer or smartphone works, but you certainly use it to send messages through the ethers. Similarly, we may only be able to think of layers and levels with the most elementary definitions of "portal" or "conduit" or "string theory" or "quantum physics," but that doesn't stop us from traveling in them!

If this is all starting to make sense to you now, or if it doesn't make sense but you're willing to hang in there and see what happens next, wonderful! For now, all you need to know is that as human beings, we still can't jump too many layers or levels. However, the majority of us can open our windows to receive Divine guidance with clarity and ease; we can jump to layers or levels that we can process and work in.

These experiences are profoundly useful to us.

As we become more and more conscious and more infused with Divine vibration, more used to transversing in these higher layers and levels, we eventually become able to connect to more expansive realms such as pure energy, Universal knowing, and Oneness.

It doesn't really matter what you can do today. Start where you are, and this will be the perfect experience for you. The Divine will arrive in the manner and method that is the easiest for you to understand.

Intuition is instantaneous

Okay, so you've asked to receive Divine guidance—your windows are open. No use running screaming around the house trying to shutter everything up now! What's done is done. That's because intuition is instantaneous—it happens beyond time, or outside of time. It happens in the moment of asking. That's why you were able to answer the question in chapter 1, even before you knew what the question was. In fact, many of you knew the answer before you even read the chapter. That's because intuitive information is instantaneous, instant, immediate, split second, same time.

Sometimes, intuition even happens before you ask! For example, if a client makes an appointment for a reading with me, I often get a sudden flood or flash of information before the session—I'll be going about my day when somebody's life story starts playing like a movie in my head. When the client shows up for their appointment, I've already received a full download of their situation. This advance information happens often enough so that now I don't worry when I'm suddenly flashing on a person I've never met! Instead, I recognize that I'm "pre-receiving" information, probably so that I can work faster and more deeply during our time together.

When you open your window to us, you also open to our further gateways, windows, doorways of understanding. This expansion is without limit.

—The Messages

Intuition is physical

In *The Messages* at the start of this chapter, the guides talked about intuition arriving as "a sense of expansion" or a "lightness on the skin." These are accurate and useful ways of describing the sensation of what it feels like during the instant you open your *window* to Divine realms. (You can read more about *The Messages* on page 6.)

Other ways of understanding this awareness might be a feeling or sensation of:

- A "hit" or "flash" or "flood" of information or emotional content
- Tingling and shimmering in the air around you
- Shuddering, shaking, body convulsing, teeth chattering
- Temperature change in your body
- The feeling of being flooded with sensation or emotion

After all, it's all about energy! As humans, we vibrate at a certain level, depending on how conscious we are and what we're experiencing that day. If you're really angry or sad, you're probably vibrating at a lower level than usual. If you're happy and blissed out, your level's a lot higher.

What's interesting to know is that every time you open your window and ask to receive intuitive information, you raise your vibration. And, as these things work, the more you raise your vibration, the easier it is to receive intuitive information.

Intuition causes vibrational shift

You know how you feel when you're around someone who's got a really high vibration? For example, imagine you get to have tea with the Dalai Lama. Before your audience, you're a bit nervous—after all, he's a super-important spiritual leader. What if he finds your questions silly, or you spill chai on his robe? But then he walks in the room, and you instantly feel fantastic. In seconds you're laughing, feeling totally blissed out, just because you're in his presence. Such is the power of the Dalai Lama, who has a very high vibration—much higher than most humans wandering around the planet.

The same happens with the etheric beings, guides, and angels who exist at a higher vibration—when you're around them, in communication with them, your vibration also raises. It's like a kind of reverse gravity—your vibration raises and holds to the highest vibration you're around.

For example, you can't match the vibration of an angel, but being around an angel will raise you to the highest vibration you can reach as a human. Any raised vibration that you experience is always perceived as love, bliss, healing, peace—one of the most enjoyable and sustaining aspects of intuitive work. You feel a sense of expansion, opening—it's the *ahhhhh* factor! It's as if suddenly everything lightens and brightens, and gets more fun, simpler, easier.

Being *aware* of this feeling of expansion and raising vibration can clue you in to when you have opened your window, and are experiencing direct connection with the Divine.

Exercise: Raise Your Vibration

Ready to raise your vibration? This exercise is very pleasant, and not a bit scary. Repeat it as often as you'd like. It's a terrific practice when you're feeling anxious, upset, angry, sad, depressed, or confused, and it's a superb way to become aware of the subtle and profound sensations that come when you connect with the Divine. Here's how:

1. Do your setup, as you did on page 13.

2. Begin to notice the energy in the room. For example, the air in front of you might feel fluttery and cool, whereas the air behind you might feel warm and happy.

3. Now, ask the Universe to help you experience energy at a higher vibration. You will notice the air in the room begin to shift, and to feel different: lighter, brighter, more expanded, luscious. Allow yourself to dissolve into the brilliant experience of this new energy. Simply lock into the hum of the Universe. You may feel a

tingling or a shimmer. Some of you may even be aware of different energy densities in the room or even sense other entities.

4. Bask in this raised vibration for a while, the same way you'd bask in warm sunlight. Feel it in on your face, arms, legs; some of you may sense your hair is standing on end. Allow your heart to open and don't be surprised if you are met with a flood of emotion, healing, love, bliss. Stay here as long as you like.

5. When you are ready to come back, say thank you to the Divine and slowly count backward from ten, as you reorient yourself to this reality and this earth life.

6. Say, "Ahhhhh!" out loud, simply because it feels good.

7. Write about what you experienced in your journal. A common observation may be that nothing happened and everything happened—both at the same time. A common observation is that you felt amazing, and you want to experience this energy again. Does it surprise you to know that the Universe is always humming, vibrating, and existing as energy in this way, even if you forget to notice?

With every infusion of Universe/Divine/One/All,
you are transformed. Even in thought—
even as you consider this idea—
your vibration is raised, shifted, opened.
—The Messages

Part Two

—◈—

Receiving

four

Knowing

Receiving is instantaneous. There is no time that you do not know, and no time that you begin to know. You know already.
—The Messages

Hey there, know-it-all! What does it feel like to grasp the secrets of the Universe and to know everything that is, all at once? I ask this, because this is what you know, in every cell of your body and in every hair on your head.

You know everything already.

Of course, this shouldn't surprise you. As you've already realized or are beginning to discover, you are 100 percent Divine, every single speck. That means you're made up of the same exact stuff and substance as the Universe. Your body, your brain, your favorite big toe—it all contains a little bit of *all that is*. Energetically, there's no difference. Thus, whenever you use intuition, there's no learning curve, time delay, or lag time—it's always instantaneous, immediate, there. Why wouldn't it be? It's your essence, your core—it's who you are. There's no separation between the Universe and you; you communicate instantaneously at all times, because *you are the same.*

In this section, we're going to cover the different ways that we receive intuitive information. Basically, without worrying too much about fancy terminology, intuition arrives in five basic ways:

- Knowing
- Sensing
- Hearing
- Seeing
- Strands

You've probably heard some different terms used for this stuff, and I'll probably use some of these terms as we move forward: claircognizance, clairaudience, and clairvoyance are a few of them. However, I like to keep things as simple as possible—there's enough to learn without tripping over tricky lexicon.

When you know, you know

Deep knowing is perhaps the most common way that most of us receive intuitive information. You may experience this method countless times during your day, without even realizing that you're doing it. In a nutshell, deep knowing is when you just know.

It's instinctive.

It's instantaneous.

It's unmistakable.

And you can always, always trust it.

We've all heard of "gut instinct," and that's one way to think about deep knowing. But what's misleading about gut instinct is this: deep knowing doesn't always hit you in the gut. In fact, it often affects many other physical locations besides your stomach. Sometimes you feel it in your brain, such as a headache. Sometimes your heart will beat faster, or your chest will feel tight, or you'll get a rush of adrenaline down your thighs, or your whole spine will flood with chills. Sometimes your hands will get shaky, or your neck will ache. Deep knowing always appears in the body but not always the stomach, as folklore suggests. For example:

- It's the "yes" you feel in your shoulders when you interview for a job and you "just know" you're going to get it (and the next day, you find out that you did).

- It's the "flash" you feel in your whole body when you buy a lottery ticket at your kid's school—and you end up winning the Year of Free Pizza.

- It's the sick feeling in the pit of your stomach when you realize, even without any real proof, that your significant other is having an affair.

Deep knowing is with us all the time, but we are often so distracted by the demands of daily life that we forget to pay attention to it. And sometimes, even if we are paying attention, we forget to trust what we receive.

You do not need to be activated, aligned, attuned.
The activation exists already. It is only that you become
aware of this activation when you open your windows.

—The Messages

The facts can mislead you

Deep knowing has nothing to do with facts, figures, and flow charts. In fact, the instantaneous intuition of deep knowing in the body often runs counter to rational, linear, left-brain thought.

Why? Well, partly it's how most of us (Americans, anyway) have been raised. From the time we enter kindergarten, we're taught to line up quietly, sit at our desks, follow the rules, and state the facts—so much so that by the time we're considered educated and ready to graduate high school, college, or beyond, we're pretty savvy little Rationalists. Dyed-in-the-wool Left-Brainers. Fact Spouters. Figure Followers.

Chart Makers. Except, of course, those of us who somehow figured out that we didn't care for facts—we preferred art. Or those who discovered we didn't particularly like figures—we enjoyed music. Or cooking. Or gardening. Or whatever it was that allowed us to stay on a lovely path of intuitive flow, all the time. We right-brain rebels rejected left-brain law, feeling more comfortable—and more competent—using another, entirely different method of brainpower.

Trendspotters such as Daniel H. Pink, the author of leading books on the power of right-brain thinking, have described the shift in our world from thinking in facts to understanding the whole truth. As Pink writes in his book *A Whole New Mind: Why Right-Brainers Will Rule the Future*, "Left-brain-style thinking used to be the driver and right-brain-style thinking the passenger. Now, R-Directed Thinking [i.e., right-brain thinking] is suddenly grabbing the wheel, stepping on the gas, and determining where we're going and how we'll get there."

It just makes sense. After all, facts can never describe or determine the whole story. Indeed, the real truth of a person, energy, or situation is always concerned with deeper meanings, emotional content, and the heart's opening. It's never solely about facts and figures.

Remember, facts are just one layer of reality. When we use intuition, we expand the number of layers we're able to work in; facts become just one part of the equation. The real truth is never based on only the rational. The real truth—the emotional truth, the soul truth—is always found in the energetic, including:

- The heart of the matter
- The truth behind the truth
- The energy of the situation
- The life lesson
- The soul lesson
- What is true for you

In deep knowing, our bodies will feel uncomfortable until we are satisfied that the deeper soul truth has been answered—that the "facts" of a situation match the energy and the emotional truth.

What deep knowing feels like

We are aware of deep knowing in our bodies—and by bodies, I mean in the entire container that we call our physical self. Deep knowing may include:

- Chills, such as an energy rush that flows fully and instantaneously up your spine, down your thighs, across your chest, etc. This may feel like a sudden flooding of energy. Sometimes people also call this Kundalini energy.

- Tingling and shimmering sensations, on the skin or in the air upon the skin.

- Twitching and shifting in the body.

- Shuddering, jerking, or uncontrolled convulsive movement. These are somewhat like energy surges and/or releases, and they can be surprising or even embarrassing, depending on where you are when they happen!

- Hair rising on your arms or back of your neck.

- Nausea, faintness, shortness of breath, heart racing, sweating, chills, shuddering, and shaking are also all common if you try to go against the "truth."

- A feeling of deep, unshakable certainty; this may feel like a sensation of groundedness, gravity, being centered, being whole, feeling expansive, at ease. You just know.

An example of deep knowing

Many years ago, I was at home preparing to go out to Thanksgiving dinner at a family friend's. At that time, my four children were ages one through seventeen, and it took quite a bit of effort to get everyone dressed in their best and out the door. The children's father had gotten everyone into the car and strapped into their car seats and so forth; everyone was waiting for me. But for some reason I was dilly-dallying in the house. For some reason, I just knew that I needed to wait. Once or twice I even opened the front door, ready to head out—but I forced myself to stay. For some reason, I knew I was supposed to wait. I knew this in the deepest part of my being.

About ten minutes later, I finally got in the car. We pulled out of the driveway and started down the block, when suddenly I had a flash or feeling of something not right. At that moment, a woman jogged past us, and for whatever reason, I was compelled to talk to her. "Ask her what she's looking for," I pleaded with my husband, and although it made no sense, he pulled over and rolled down the window.

"He's gone, he's gone," the woman stammered, her voice filled with pain and fear, and ran on hysterically. In a flood of feeling that I cannot describe, I saw, felt, and knew everything.

"He's in the creek," I said frantically. "It's a little boy, and he's in the creek!" Seeing the look on my face, my husband didn't even question me. He raced the car to where a large run-off creek ran behind the neighborhood, about six blocks away. With every passing second, I was possessed more acutely with dread—the feeling was so intense that I could hardly breathe; my whole body felt suffocated, as if I were gasping for air. "Hurry! Hurry!" shouted through my mind, as the car raced forward.

When we reached the creek we saw him immediately, standing in the rushing water: a little boy of about four, already up to his thighs in the cold stream, headed toward deep water. He was so cold he was gray, and he had a look on his face of absolute stillness.

My husband leapt from the car and pulled the boy from the water, shouting for help.

Within seconds, a search party of people came running toward them. They told us later that the boy had severe autism; he'd wandered off and somehow made his way to the creek. As they bundled him up in blankets and carried him away, I realized that my whole body was shaking in shock.

I knew without doubt that if we'd pulled out of our driveway even a few minutes earlier, we'd have never seen the woman jogger, never discovered the boy in the creek. It would have been too late.

This entire event happened many years ago, before I understood what intuition was or how to use it. At that time, I had no idea I would eventually open as a psychic. Yet, even then, my sense of deep knowing was fully activated, as it is for everyone.

If you are faced with an emergency such as this example, your reaction will be strong, clear, and real. The more serious the situation, the more intense the deep knowing will be. If you feel this happening to you, pay attention and act as you are directed to.

Trusting deep knowing

Because deep knowing is instantaneous and held in the body, it's one of the easiest forms of intuition to receive. However, it can be the hardest to trust as information, because it's merely a physical sensation.

That's why I always check my deep knowing with another technique.

For example, say I start with deep knowing—the flash or flood that I receive in my whole body. Next, I'll double-check it with another psychic technique, such as psychic hearing (clairaudience), psychic seeing (clairvoyance), or other methods that we'll be covering soon. I like to check with different techniques, because even though I trust, it helps me understand the situation more fully.

Recently I was asked by the local newspaper to provide some psychic forecasts. One of the questions they asked was if the Oregon Ducks, the local college football team that was having a particularly stellar season, would win the national college football championship.

Gulp! 'Round here, this is Ducks country—and I really didn't want to predict that the Ducks would lose. With great trepidation, I set about trying to determine the game winner, and there it was: a huge flash of deep knowing—the Ducks will lose.

I trusted that first flash—I always do. But I really needed to hear, or see, or understand it a different way. So I started using other methods in my tool kit: psychic hearing, psychic seeing. I immediately began to "see" a player in my mind, down on one knee, while at the same time I heard the word *kick*. With this extra information, it all came together:

I clearly realized that the Ducks would lose, and it was related to a guy down on one knee.

A week later, they did lose, due to an unbelievable field goal by the opposing team in the last few moments of overtime.

I was not popular with Ducks fans—and I was very glad I had checked, and double-checked, my deep knowing with other techniques.

Exercise: Divine Truth

1. Write down ten things you've been told or that you know about yourself, that you believe are "right," such as "I'm generous" or "I'm clumsy" or "I'm a great dancer." Ask yourself, "Is this true for me?" Let your body inform you what is or is not true. Be surprised by what you learn.

2. Over the next week, carry a notebook with you. Every time you have a sense of deep knowing such as a flash, hit, back chill, shuddering, deep certainty, or any other way you experience deep knowing, write it down. As time passes and what you have "known" comes into reality, return to this notebook and notice how deep knowing is always, infallibly true.

Every way that you receive is correct; there is no right way. There is only awakening to the awareness that you, the other, are One. You understand, because you are the same.

—The Messages

---

five

Sensing

*The energy that you sense—this represents only one layer
of density. You, as human, can sense a range of densities.
For many of you, this range is expanding.*

—The Messages

Last week, while working at my Portland office, I discovered a miracle
on my calendar: a full forty minutes of unclaimed time. Now, Portland
is a wonderful city, filled with delightful places to explore . . . but lately
my client schedule has been so full, I've been driving to my office, working nonstop, and then driving straight home. Needless to say, I was
excited about this unexpected forty minutes suddenly presenting itself
like a sparkly jewel. In fact, I was almost giddy.

Coffee at a café?

Bookstore browsing?

Shopping?

So many choices!

I headed out into the beautiful fall day and immediately was captivated by the energetic vibration of the air surrounding me. It was as if

all the trees and plants had decided to give off extra oxygen all at once. It was a "vibe" of luscious green, a sweetly rich energy that seemed to be covering my skin and hair in an almost magical way.

On a whim, I ducked into the corner toy store—the kind where all the toys are from Europe and everything's out of the box, waiting to be played with. A trio of twenty-somethings was standing near a display counter laughing hysterically, as they tossed some kind of bouncy ball that was designed to bounce at random. Sure enough, it bounced right over and hit me randomly (but softly!) in the face. I was startled, then started laughing too. A customer who'd seen what had happened started laughing, as did her child. As did the store owner behind the counter. Seven beings, suddenly crazy with laughter at this silly bouncy ball— and, of course, the vibration, the energy, the vibe was also bouncing off the walls.

It was a bona fide Bliss Fest.

Vibrationally, it was lively, warm, uplifting, transcendent—and it felt marvelous. Once we'd stopped laughing, I went to look at toys farther back in the store, and the *vibe* trailed after me like a golden cloud. Passing the twenty-somethings on their way out, we all beamed at each other like giant rays of sunshine.

This is the kind of vibe or energy that is created when you laugh, play, act silly, roll around on the lawn, enjoy, and fully connect with others from a place where your heart is open. This vibe happens when we least expect it—when we unexpectedly let our inner child, as well as our own inner adult—vibrate out to the world.

I say *inner adult*, because so often we are so busy inhabiting our highest selves that we forget to share this lovely, glowing, beaming self with others. Perhaps we are afraid if we reveal this Divine, radiant inner self that others won't understand us. Perhaps we are afraid they will reject us, or think we're weird.

Of course, there's nothing further from the truth.

The Divine is infectious, because it's what we all are.

When we connect from a place of high vibration, all the aspects that might normally separate us, such as culture, beliefs, appearance, sex, age, wealth, and the other myriad aspects of our bodies or "physical containers" simply disappear.

When you begin to experience the Divine realm more frequently,
you will learn to identify what it feels like to shift from one
energetic realm to another.

—The Messages

Gauging vibration with color and words

When you first enter a room or space, you sense its intrinsic *vibe* or energy. If you are busy, distracted, running around on a tight schedule, you may not pay attention to this very carefully—you may bluster your way forward, concentrating on the task at hand, without really noticing the vibration that surrounds you.

Yet if you take a moment and detach from all the busyness around you, this energy is incredibly easy to sense and evaluate.

Color is one way I like to rate vibration. The color itself isn't really the point—it's just a way of differentiating between one thing and another. But if you can begin to gauge the energy in one room as "orange" and in another room as "blue," you learn how to differentiate between different energy sensations—you'll start to understand that the energies or *vibe* of the two rooms is qualitatively different.

Using words as descriptors is another useful way of differentiating whether energy is high or low vibration. For example, when you sense a person, place, thing, or idea, try to describe it using words. It is:

- Musty
- Floaty
- Dull
- Sacred
- Sad
- Serene

- Earthy
- Airy
- Sustaining
- Mystical

I don't know about you, but if I have a choice between musty and mystical, I'm always gonna head for that higher vibe!

How to gauge *vibration*

Try it yourself. The next time you come across a place, person, or idea, immediately assign it a color and word. For example, if you said, "Blue, cool," I'd guess you were in a serene place, the way you might feel in an ancient church. If you said, "Green, lively," I'd expect you to be in a natural setting, flush with trees and nature.

Again, the actual colors or words you choose don't really matter. You can say, "Tangerine with a splash of plum and a basenote of evergreen" or "Yellow and buzzy." It doesn't matter. The whole idea is for you to begin differentiating, so you have a way of labeling energy and holding its vibrational level in your mind.

Once you're able to gauge the energy for a person, place, thing, or idea, you'll also start noticing the different energy pockets in that field. For example, say you're gauging the energy in your living room. Can you sense these smaller energy patches? Walk around from one area of the room to another, and just gauge how the energy changes from space to space. Now, feng shui experts might suggest you declutter any areas in a room that are presenting as "red, 1, cluttered" to get the energy moving at a higher vibration—and I'm all for that.

But I'll also suggest that, without lifting a finger, you can simply ask the energy to shift. After all, you're Divine energy. The energetic vibration in your living room (or in any person, place, thing, or idea) is too. There's no separation between you.

So go ahead. Sense the energy's distinctive, differentiated quality. Then, simply ask, suggest, or request that it raise to a higher level. You may feel like magically waving your hands about, too, just to add emphasis—but it's not necessary. Crazy as it sounds, you'll immediately feel the energy relaxing, easing, shifting, and raising *vibration*, from the moment you ask. Pretty nifty, huh?

Everything is energetic

I used the example of your living room, but as you well know, everything holds vibration. This includes:

- You

- Every other person on this planet

- Animals, trees, nature, and all sentient beings on Earth

- All inanimate objects (which also hold vibration) such as rocks, wood, water, sky

- All organizations, including businesses, groups, cultures, countries, nations, etc.

- Ideas, concepts, and thoughts

- Energies, entities, and spirits from the other realms

- Everything in the Universe

- The relationships between all these things

- And the list goes on!!

It's easy to sense the vibration of a person or place—in most cases, we just "know" it. But objects are also rich with energy—and we can read this energy as vibration, too. Take a moment now, and gauge the objects nearby. The coffee cup you're drinking from. The sofa you're sitting on. The floor beneath your feet.

Now, look out a window and notice the energy of the urban or natural setting that's in your view. An urban setting, with all its gray concrete and busy hum of people, has a certain kind of vibe. How would you color and rate it? The rustle of trees on a summer day has a certain kind of vibration that can be magical; how do you color and/or rate these?

You'll soon notice that some objects or "Universes" don't vibrate very high: they cause you to close down and feel angry, numb, and stressed.

Others vibrate very high, causing your heart to soar with openness, love, bliss.

Go one step further, and choose an object to hold in your hand. For example, you might pick up a small statue of an elephant, a tiny wooden thing that you've had since you were a kid. Maybe your mom gave it to you—you can't quite remember. Take a moment, and hold that object in your hand. Gauge it by color, word. For a moment, also allow the emotional content or the "story" of that object to come in to your awareness. (We'll do more of this later.)

In the case of this elephant, you might rate it a "green, fun." But you may also notice that it contains emotional qualities such as comfort, childhood, mother, playing, etc. It may even conjure up scenes from the past, when you were a child playing with the elephant.

If you haven't sensed energy in objects before, you may experience some emotional overload—all this energetic information, all this vibrational range, right here in the room with you! Suddenly, things may seem very, very crowded.

Just breathe, and understand that you are experiencing a shift in consciousness. What you are experiencing is not new; the energy has been there all the time. It's simply the first time you have sensed it, or the first time you sensed it this deeply.

Finally, there are other energetic objects that are bigger, more Universal. These may include galaxies, planets, and so on. These are "Universes" within bigger infinite Universes. These also have energetic vibration.

Choose your vibration

Once you realize that all objects have vibration, you may very quickly decide that you don't want that energy in your home or space.

That old bathrobe from your ex? Outta here.

The mug from the place you worked five years ago? Ditch it.

The table passed down from your very crotchety great aunt? Craigslist, please.

And so on.

In my own home I am so sensitive to the energy of objects that I don't keep very much "stuff." This is quite difficult in a family of "savers," but too much "stuff" makes me cranky. I find particular joy in things that are natural, such as a bowl of rocks collected on the beach in Washington—the vibration is neutral and calm. Other things are positive, such as a crystal lamp that once belonged to my grandmother; I feel happy having that by my bedside.

Sometimes when I'm at other people's homes, I am stunned by the amount of "stuff" they have. Oh sure, it's great stuff—I guess. But I myself can't live with that many objects, that much extra. The energy gets too dense.

If you are looking for a quick way to raise vibration, consider clearing your environment. There are plenty of great books on feng shui out there, but mostly the key is to keep items that make your heart soar—and chuck, give away, or sell what makes you feel low. Once you start gauging, it's simple to know which is which.

I am well aware that some people are "tossers" and some people are "savers." If you are a tosser, it is easy to keep your space energetically clear. If you are a saver, I invite you to reconsider the energy you surround yourself with, and to get rid of anything that is negative or low vibration.

Exercise: Raising Vibration

Try your hand at assessing the vibrational range of places, spaces, and people. If you feel called to do so, ask the vibe to shift to a higher level. Notice what happens.

1. Every time you enter a new space, take a moment to sense the energy or vibe.

2. Begin to notice vibration in nature. On a walk in the woods, for example, sense where the energy is more dense, more light, more compelling.

3. When you travel, notice how different types of areas vibrate: ocean, mountains, desert, and meadows, for instance, all carry

different vibration and different emotional content for you. Write down what you notice.

4. Practice gauging and shifting the vibration in people. Simply note the core vibration of whomever you come across, and then ask, request, or suggest that they raise it. Do this by closing your eyes and telepathically sending them the message "I invite you to raise your vibration." Notice what happens: instantly, within a few hours, within a few days.

We say: energy differs according to vibrational quality.
By this you are able to differentiate, to resonate,
and, eventually, to raise.

—The Messages

---

six

Signs, Synchronicities & Strands

We are communicating with you constantly and continually. Look around you at all times. Listen with your heart open. There is no time we are not in full communication with you, guiding you on your soul's path.
—The Messages

Is the Universe random? From what I have seen in my years on this earth, the signs, synchronicities, and strands we experience when we are paying attention are too consistently well-timed and welcome to be anything but Divinely orchestrated.

I cannot imagine that the Universe is random, because as I've begun to explore intuition firsthand, I've learned that when you delve deep—when you systematically (a) ask for guidance, (b) allow yourself to receive it, and (c) begin to take actions toward manifesting or creating that guidance—well, things start to work in your favor more quickly than you might guess. It's a kind of turbocharged "yes" from the Universe that even a cynic would have a tough time disregarding. For example:

I can't find it random that after weeks of indecision, I wake up one morning and just know that today is the day to list my car on Craigslist. That morning! No waiting around! Do it! I post a listing, and within five minutes I have an email from a potential buyer. The very next day, I sell my car to that same buyer, for $400 above my asking price.

Really.

Random? Coincidental? Well, maybe, if it were just this one thing. But of course, there's more . . .

- I can't find it random that while paying monthly bills, I notice my bank balance is at an uncomfortably low point. Feeling confident in the Divine's ability to correct this situation, I say aloud, "Universe, I'd really love to have some extra cash." Within twenty-four hours, a high-paying project arrives in my lap. Out of nowhere. The Universe delivers what we need, when we need it.

- I can't find it random that during meditation, I see the face of my Beloved in my mind's eye every day for weeks—even though I won't meet him until six or seven months later. The Universe clues us in.

- I can't find it random that while spreading my father's ashes on a deserted beach on Puget Sound, I look up and see a gigantic bald eagle perched less than thirty feet above me. The bald eagle stands sentry for a full twenty minutes, as I complete my ceremony. I know it is a message from my father. The Universe helps us heal.

- I can't find it random when a client, on the spur of the moment, asks if I have time to see her adult daughter. The impromptu reading I do for the daughter is life-changing; she emails me later that it sets her on an extraordinary new course that she'd never dreamed possible. The Universe knows when it's time to connect.

- I can't find it random that in meditation I communicate for the first time with Merlin—(yes, that Merlin). The experience is profound, and I know that there is more to come. The very next day,

I see a book on the laundry room floor that I've never seen before. The book is entitled *Merlin*. The Universe knows the next step.

Learning to follow

Walking the intuitive path when you're paying attention to signs, synchronicities, and strands is like traveling a popular hiking trail managed by the U.S. Forest Service—it's especially well traveled and well marked.

If you can't find a park ranger, there's going to be a sign. Or if you can't find a sign, at least you can count on another hiker showing up on the path—someone who has a compass that points true north. You'd never expect, on this kind of well-marked trail, to have to go it alone.

It works the same way when you're following the signs, synchronicities, and strands of the Universe, too—you never have to worry about getting lost, running into a bear, or landing in a clump of poison oak. You're always directed. You're always headed the right way. You always know which way to turn.

Of course, you can choose to ignore the signs, synchronicities, and strands that present themselves at every fork in the road! In fact, countless millions of people decide to do this, every single second of every single day! There they are, marching along the hiking trails of life with no more than a tube of ChapStick and a water bottle, navigating with no help from the Divine whatsoever, thank you very much.

Hey . . . that's one way to work your life path.

But be forewarned that when we traipse out into the wilderness of life alone without Divine guidance leading the way, chances are good that we're going to get lost. Now, getting lost is okay now and then. Sometimes getting lost is part of the journey.

But when we're actively trying not to get lost—when we're trying to stay on the highest possible path for us at this time—why on earth would we refuse Divine information?

Get lost long enough, or get lost badly enough, and most of us seem to figure out that traveling without Divine guidance doesn't really work. Finally, we let go of our stubbornness, our bravado, our ego, and become humble/brave/smart enough to start receiving, following, and trusting the cosmos.

Once you take this step for yourself, it gets pretty easy to look around and see which of your fellow travelers are following signs, synchronicities, and strands, too—and who's still out wandering in circles. One glance, and you'll easily spot:

- The person who is miserable at their job—but is afraid to quit
- The person who is unhappy in their marriage—but won't take steps to make things better
- The person who uses drugs, alcohol, cigarettes, food, shopping, pornography, gambling, sex, or other addictions to self-medicate their emotional pain
- The person who worries constantly about getting sick, or losing all their money, or losing their relationship—and then does
- And so on

Of course, these types of people are continually receiving signs, synchronicities, and strands just like anyone else on this planet. But often, they're so distracted by their emotional pain that they don't see what's right in front of them.

If you haven't been aware of signs, synchronicities, and strands, you'll be quite surprised to know how much Divine guidance is actually being beamed down to Earth (so to speak) all the time. And once you start paying attention, you'll be shocked at how actively the Universe is working to guide, help, and direct you, 24/7!

How do they work?

When you know what each of these Universal communiqués looks like, you can identify them faster—and follow them more quickly. Ideally, you'll be able to clearly categorize what's a sign, what's a synchronicity, and what's a strand, so that when one appears in front of you, you can quickly say, "Oh, that is so obviously a sign" and then follow it. Or you can say, "Ahh, definitely a synchronicity" and pay attention to what's next, or "Oh, a strand is at work," and then follow it further.

Signs, synchronicities, and strands always lead us in the direct of our highest possibility—they are ways that the Universe attempts to get our attention. Ideally, when you receive a sign, synchronicity, or strand, you will immediately recognize that you are receiving Divine guidance, and start following it!

What do *signs* look like?

Signs often quite literally look like signs. They may be an actual sign, such as a billboard, street sign, or banner in front of a store. Or they may be smaller signs such as written messages, including:

- A letter
- A brochure
- A book or phrase in a book
- A news article (paper or online)
- A website
- An email
- And so on

Signs can also be other common methods of electronic communication, such as:

- A phone call
- Something on the radio, iPod, or any form of auditory electronic media
- Something on TV, a DVD, Hulu, YouTube, or any form of visual electronic media
- Anything on a computer, smartphone, or any form of electronic communication
- Other ways we haven't thought of yet that are well beyond electronica!

If there's a method of communication, whether an older form such as smoke signals or Morse code or a newer form such as smartphones (or whatever the newest thing is at the time you're reading this), the Divine will use it to send you messages. Why? It's just easier that way. You're already used to looking at and listening to these sources—so the Divine can trust that you're paying at least some amount of attention!

What do synchronicities look like?

Basically, they look pretty much the same as signs, but they're more to do with the people around you and how the Universe arranges and orchestrates chance meetings, chance communications, that kind of thing.

For example, you know you're experiencing a synchronicity when one of the first things you say is, "Fancy meeting you here!" or "What a coincidence!" Here are a few true-life examples from folks I know:

- Your smartphone "butt dials" a business associate you've been trying to reach for three weeks—but haven't been able to connect with. The recipient answers miraculously on the first ring, and you set up a meeting for the very next day. *Yes!*

- You need one last class for the semester, but nothing fits your schedule. Finally, you find an odd class in modern dance that will work—it's literally the only other class left. You don't know anything about modern dance, but you want to get your credits, so you sign up anyway. Ten minutes into this class, you realize that you have found your Life's Path. Gracias, Universe!

- You have a carefully planned itinerary, but one that doesn't allow for missed planes. Unfortunately, you have just missed yours and have to wait three hours for the next flight. You set your bags down next to an attractive man, and during the wait you start talking. Curiously, you find your seats are located exactly next to each other on the plane. By the end of the flight, you've exchanged phone numbers. But the end of the month, you're married. Universal champagne all around!

- You are looking for a space to do some creative exploration, you have only a tiny budget for rent. You've been dilly-dallying about finding a space, but one day you wake up and decide to go looking. For whatever reason, you feel compelled to grab a cup of coffee at a café you don't usually frequent before you start hunting. Sure enough, an acquaintance is at the café; you haven't seen her in months. You tell her your quest, and she says, "Oh, I have some space downtown." Wow! What a coincidence! You go and look, and it's perfect! You ask how much, and she agrees to $200 a month—about half of what you were expecting to pay. Thank you, Divine!

All of the above happened, because of the marvelous way the Divine has of pulling strings, throwing out signs, setting up synchronicities, fixing schedules, and notifying us of what we're supposed to be doing next via intuitive messages, 24/7.

In asking, the window is opened. With intent, the door swings clear. When you are ready, and even in those times when you do not understand you are ready, we wait upon you.

—The Messages

Strands

Strands are like the clues on your life-path map.

Hmmm . . . does this mean all you have to do is follow along the clearly marked path, and you'll come to the treasure lickety split? Bring your shovel?

Unfortunately, it's a bit more of process.

Sigh.

It's always a process, isn't it?

For reasons known only to the Divine, you don't get your whole Personal Life Path all at once. Instead, you get a little piece of it. This little piece of information is what I call a strand, a clue, something to follow.

The process of following strands might best be likened to a scavenger hunt—you know, the kind where you race to find the secret note in the hollow of the old oak tree; then when you crack that clue, you race to the wishing well for the next clue; then you hurry to the rain barrel for the next clue, and so on. In general:

1. You don't get the whole map all at once.

2. You only get the next clue or strand.

3. A strand is a piece or a part of the information you need to complete the next step.

4. Once you get to that next step, you wait for the next strand.

Strands at work

Let's take a look at an example of how noticing signs and synchronicities and then following them as strands might be brilliantly executed, in chronological order.

1. You are tired, burnt out, and want a new job—or at least a vacation.

2. Driving home from work, a billboard shouts, "Paris, $399." *Mais oui!*

3. The next day, you're reading the newspaper and notice a meeting about traveling in France. You decide to attend.

4. At the meeting, someone hands you a "random" brochure on Spain. You toss it in the recycling.

5. That night, you dream about Spain in vivid detail; you can't get it out of your mind.

6. Two days later, you receive an email about a workshop being held in Barcelona, which you delete.

7. Five minutes later, you receive an email from a friend who somehow heard about the workshop in Barcelona, and will you please go with her?

8. As you read her email, you suddenly remember your dream. In that moment, you are overwhelmed with every detail of it. You suddenly have an intuitive *A-ha!* moment, and realize you have been receiving signs and synchronicities about Spain! And you're actually in the middle of following a strand!

9. The Universe laughs, shaking its head at why it took you so long.

10. You get on the phone and reserve your workshop spot and ticket.

11. Two months later, while at the Barcelona workshop, you meet an ex-pat now living in Spain.

12. You hit it off so well that you become business partners. You can't believe it's happening so fast, but all systems are go!

13. You quit your job, move your business to Spain over the next year, and enjoy unprecedented growth. You couldn't imagine a more interesting job, or place to live, or better life.

14. Looking back, you are stunned by how simply everything happened and are dazzled by the strands held out to you by the Universe.

U-turns allowed

Did you notice how in the above example you didn't even realize you were following signs, synchronicities, and strands until about half of the way through? If we are not paying close attention to intuitive information, this is often how it goes!

We miss signs.

We refuse synchronicities.

We skip strands.

We literally block, refuse, or get in the way of Divine guidance trying to show us the way, multiple times. Poor Universe! This is how it goes so many times.

And yet, in the above situation . . .

The Universe persevered. It continued to stay stubbornly by your side, sending repeated signs and synchronicities about Spain, hoping to get your attention so you'd follow along on the strand for a while, and end up with your dream job.

And eventually you did.

Oh sure, it took quite a bit of Universal effort—sometimes that's what it takes for some of us more stubborn folks—but over time, you figured it out: "Hey, I'm getting signs. Hey, I'm getting synchronicities. Hey, maybe I'll just follow along on this intuitive strand for a while, and see where it leads."

Whenever you see signs start to show up in multiple, or synchronicities start to cluster, start paying attention. The Universe is dangling an active intuitive strand right in front of you—and following it will take you to a marvelous treasure indeed!

If you are a person running around with your nose to the grindstone, constantly maxing out your schedule and checking your Facebook status, you may not find it easy to spot strands at first. But if you're a person who is aware that intuitive information is all around us, that the Divine is working in our favor, and that the Universe is without limits—well, then you will easily notice these signs, synchronicities, and strands, and be able to follow them to their lovely conclusion.

Which is your highest possibility.

And that has quite a nice ring to it.

Exercise: Cosmic Convergences

1. Take a look at the major events in your life—when you met your true love, when you got that perfect job, moments when your life changed for the better. Now, backtrack, and write down all the signs and synchronicities that set you on a course for this outcome. Are you surprised to see how the Divine led you from one strand to the next?

2. Think of all the recent occasions when you seemed to be "led" or "guided" by signs and synchronicities to be in the right place at the right time. Write down the sequence of events.

3. Look at what you are trying to create in your life now. Ask the Divine—in meditation, prayer, or simply by saying, "Please help me"—to reveal the next intuitive strand you need. Over the next few days, watch what happens. If you notice a strand, follow it until it leads to the next, and the next.

4. Be amazed that the Divine is an active force working in your life, at all moments and in all situations.

When you begin to understand how much we create for you,
and how actively, you will be stunned
by what you have missed before,
and what you now understand.

—The Messages

seven

Hearing

We come to you in the ways that you can understand. Your lexicon,
your logos, the sound, the sentence, the song, the word, the sign.
In all of these, we select meaning carefully.

—The Messages

Years ago, an artist friend gifted me with a card pack she'd created, called "Lexicon."[1] It was an amazing work—a gorgeous collection of illustrations, each paired with a word. It's hard to describe how lovely the artwork was, but words themselves will give you an idea. Some of them included:

- hover
- linger
- wait
- speculate

---

1. *Lexicon,* artwork by Georgiana Nehl and Lynda Lowe. Online at www.lyndalowe
   .com/image_cat.php?cat_id=18.

- conundrum

- listen

- impetus

- primal

and my personal favorite:

- palimpsest[2]

Now, these aren't your run-of-the-mill "creativity pack" words. No, these words describe some of the specific emotional reactions or states of being that we experience when we are ready to engage with our lives on a deeper level—when we are ready for soul growth. These are words that define what we feel when we are ready take our next step on our life's path.

Of course, a next step is different for each person. For example, if you've been spending days in an urban environment, the next step on your life path may be that you escape the concrete jungle. A word to help you identify this need may be *primal*, as in "You need to get out in nature and go primal."

Or, if you're a person with workaholic tendencies, always running around on a schedule without stopping to reflect if what you are creating is actually meaningful, the word that may guide you best is *listen*, as in "You may need to listen more, and talk and do less."

Or, if you're a person who will benefit from going deeper and savoring a situation, relationship, or place, instead of just skimming through it—well, your word might be *linger*, as in "You will do best if you linger within for a while." And so forth.

Words are containers of meaning. Like tiny, unique boxes that contain specific information and emotion, words allow us to understand all the nuances of growth in our life.

---

2. Defined as "a manuscript written over a partly erased older manuscript so that the old words can be read under the new."

We come also to you in thought, which is an inner hearing.
You will recognize our voices inside your head. This is our own voice,
sent to you in a manner you can understand.

—The Messages

A lexicon of meaning

There's a quote in *The Essence of the Bhagavad Gita* that "the invention of writing was not a sign of civilization's advancement, but of a decline in human awareness that made it necessary to record thoughts in written form."[3]

Wow. Writing as a sign of decline in evolution? How could that be?

And then I got it. Spirit guides, ascended masters, angels, and the like—they don't need words to communicate with each other. They communicate telepathically, in pure energy and love. The information they are required to know is simply known to them; they communicate to each other effortlessly and instantaneously, because they are One.

We lowly humans are also One. But sometimes we forget this is so.

We're getting there, and all of you who are studying intuition are making progress indeed. But right now, we still need our lexicon, our logos, our language, our lingo—symbolic combinations of even smaller symbols, sentences made of words made of letters. Right now, that's one of the easiest ways our brains think.

And if lexicon is what the Divine needs in order to work with us—well, that's what they'll use! Remember, the Divine reaches us where we are. If words are the best, easiest, fastest way for us to receive intuitive information, then words are what we will receive.

On the psychic path, it's most common for us to receive words in our mind's ear, or through psychic hearing.

---

3. Paramhansa Yogananda, *The Essence of the Bhagavad Gita: Explained by Paramhansa Yogananda, as Remembered by His Disciple, Swami Kriyananda.* Nevada City, CA: Crystal Clarity Publishers, 2008, 2.

Types of psychic hearing

The proper term for receiving intuitive words and sounds is *clairaudience*. However, because this term is difficult to remember, I often just say psychic hearing, inner hearing, receiving in words, receiving in sound, and so on . . . no need to complicate the issue with fancy lingo!

However, if you need an official definition, here it is:

Clairaudienc.e: A method of receiving Divine information through inner or outer voice, words, phrase, text, song, sound, sign, or music.

Here is a look at some of the most common clairaudient methods you may experience:

A voice in your head

This is one of the easiest ways for the Divine to reach you, and it's the one that most folks have trouble trusting. "But isn't it my own thoughts in my head?" or "What if I'm just making this up?" are two of the most common questions I'm asked at workshops and in training sessions.

Well, I could spend a lot of time and effort trying to convince you that you can trust the information you receive in psychic hearing, and that it is not made up, not your own thoughts, and that it comes from a Divine source that is not you . . . or, you can simply wait and experience this for yourself.

Trust is one of those things that you can't "get" until you "get it." And once you do "get it"? You've got it forever!

If you're not sure that the words or voices you are hearing in your head, or in what I call your mind's ear, are real, then let yourself not trust it for now. Be an unbeliever! As you open to psychic hearing more and more, you'll begin to understand how it works. And you'll come to trust, over time. That said:

- If you hear a voice in your head that sounds like something better, more advanced, more loving, or more Divine than your usual run-of-the-mill thoughts, and this Divine voice says, "You should move to Australia" or "Your true love is in that café," then please—trust this voice.

- If you hear a voice in your head that is providing advanced spiritual or metaphysical information that you have never heard before, or never even thought about, then please—trust this voice.

- If you hear a voice in your head that tells you what you really know in your body, your heart, and your soul, even though your brain has been trying to convince you otherwise, then please— trust this voice!

Again, most people hear this voice in their mind's ear, so at first you may mistake this for your own thoughts. But listen a little closer, and check out the quality of the message. If it's Divine, you'll know it.

For example, this morning I was taking a shower, when I suddenly heard a male voice resonating inside my head. I had been thinking about the concept of manifesting and creating reality and how it all worked, just turning that idea over in my mind, looking for a new way of thinking about it or teaching it.

As I stood under the warm water, I heard the phrase "Be the Dream." The sentence was repeated slowly, carefully, as if to make sure I would hear it correctly. Then, as I shampooed and rinsed, I experienced a download of understanding, in which everything became crystal clear: I understood, in a whole new way, that in order to manifest or create our reality, all we need do is be the dream that we wish to create—to exist fully, to embody all characteristics of to "be here now" in all aspects of our dream. Simply by "being" what we wish to become, our dream arrives immediately, or with sudden alacrity, into our field of awareness.

Of course, I've known about manifesting before, and many others have discussed it.

But this time, I understood it in an entirely new way. The voice I heard in my head gave me not just words, but an entire embedded meaning that was at once beyond comprehension and entirely simple. "Be the Dream" may seem redundant or unimportant to someone else, but to me it was a major *A-ha!* It pointed me in a new direction, worthy of exploration.

And I heard about it through clairaudience, in my mind's ear.

Recognizing different voices

The voices you hear in psychic hearing are most often the voices of ascended beings, including spirit guides, angels, ascended masters, saints, and Holy Ones. We're going to learn more specifically about these Divine folk in chapter 9. But until then, you can begin to recognize them and their messages:

- By vibration
- By characteristic
- By telepathy
- As voices outside your head
- As words in your head
- As electronic messaging

By vibration

Because the vibration of the beings and entities who are working with you varies from being to being, they will also sound different, or have a different "flavor" when you hear from them. For example, an angel will sound different from a spirit guide, who will sound different from the departed. Again, it's not so much about what particular messages you hear in your mind's ear; it's more of a knowing or recognizing of their different vibrational presence—the same way you've learned to differentiate the energies of people, places, spaces, things, and ideas, as we did earlier.

If you were gauging it as we did earlier with colors and words, for example, angels might be white, dazzling. Spirit guides might be purple, expansive. Ascended masters or Holy Ones might be golden, bliss-filled. If you were gauging the departed, one might be green, love-based. Another departed might be blue, sad.

Mostly, you'll just know that one spirit guide is different from another, in the same easy and natural way you know that one human being is different from another. You will recognize each being as unique, and hear each voice as unique.

By characteristic

Aside from vibrational differences, many of the entities who work with you may have unique speech characteristics, such as vocal tone, language pattern, accents, and more. This can actually get pretty funny! I mean, you could potentially have a guide who's got a Scottish burr, and another who's from the Bronx! It's possible—and I'm sure that somewhere out there, someone reading this is slapping their hand to their forehead and saying, "Why, that's what I've got!" I don't know why the Divine needs accents—again, I think it's just so that we can more easily relate to them. Plus, it's fun, and the Divine does like to have fun.

In my own experience, one of my main guides, Hajam, has an Indian accent; he's very droll, makes a lot of silly jokes, and as far as I can tell, dances around in celebration the whole livelong day, either cheering me on or teasing me! Yet another of my guides, Constance, is plainspoken, Quaker-proper, no nonsense—certainly no dancing! Conversely, when I hear from angels or ascended masters or spiritual teachers, there's no accent at all (and they certainly aren't making dumb jokes!). This group seems to be partly speaking, partly sending messaging in telepathy.

Just as each person has different characteristics, so do the guides.

By telepathy

For many people, "hearing" from their guides is a kind of "thinking" of the voice—what I would call a telepathy or thought transference. You don't really "hear" words, but you do understand meaning in the same way you would if you heard words spoken to you.

Two of my guides, Ragnar and Ashkar—spiritual masters who are extremely tall, pale, luminous beings—rarely "speak" in a voice that has any characteristic. It's definitely telepathy—I don't hear any words, yet I fully understand what is being "said" and its meaning. I don't hear the language, but I receive the content. The best way I can explain it is that I receive the voice as a kind of telepathy—rather than hearing words in my inner ear, I hear meaning.

As voices outside your head

Occasionally, some of you will hear voices outside of your head. This can be a little disconcerting—it's not a method I enjoy very much. In fact, I've asked my guides a few times to please, just let me go along quietly with interior voice! If an outer voice happens to you, and it bothers you, simply ask your guides to speak internally to you instead. They want to meet you where you are most comfortable.

However, if you're a brave being who doesn't mind outer voices, have at it. The Divine will find it interesting to work in this way, if it is the easiest way for you.

As words in your head

If you're a writer or word aficionado, the Divine will use this! Instead of hearing a word in your head, the Divine will show it to you in written form. This might look like a giant word in big letters, or a ticker tape in you mind's eye. Or, you might see printed words, or typed words, as an image in your head. Sometimes, I'll see a word in my head, and then for emphasis, they'll "highlight" it! Usually, word communication is short and sweet—I think it may be complicated for us to read long texts with our inner minds. For example, when I am doing readings and looking for fast information, I frequently see the word *Yes* in my inner mind, or the Universal sign for *No*, a circle with a big line through it. Or, I might see short phrases like "Go forward" or "Don't stop."

Occasionally, I will simply see single, emphatic words such as *Blue* or *Scout* or *Father*, which will end up being umbrella words for the reading. Because words are containers for shades and nuances of meaning, they may have double meaning; they may be symbolic; they may be a person's name; they may relate to something. For example, "blue" may mean the name Mr. Blue, or may mean a person feeling sad and blue, or may mean the color blue, or may mean something that is blue—such as the ocean, sky, bluebells, and so on.

As electronic messaging

Our guides find it very easy to send us messaging "over the wires," and of course "wirelessly." This includes things that come via electronic sources, such as a song on the radio, newscast, website, etc. This also includes phone calls, emails, text—any kind of words, sounds, and messages that are sent via what my guides call "electronica": basically, anything that's wireless or sent through the ethers. These might include:

- Phone calls, emails, texts—any kind of electronica that uses messaging, sound, or words
- Signs, such as billboards, street signs, license plates, and the like
- Words you read in a book, magazine, newspaper; for instance, when you walk into a bookstore, see a book on the table, open it at random, and the sentence you read is exactly and precisely meaningful to your situation
- Any longer texts or channeled writing that may arrive to you

Not really electronic, but also common methods are:

- Overheard conversation
- Something someone tells you directly; this could even be people you don't really know, such as the service person who comes to fix your furnace, a waiter, a grocery clerk, etc.

A word of caution

A final note about hearing "voices" either inside or outside your head: If you're hearing anything disturbing, evil, or ugly—please know that this isn't the Divine. Universal guidance is never cruel, belittling, mean, or oppressive. It is always and only uplifting, benevolent, helpful, and centered in the vibration of love.

Furthermore, if you have any history of depression, anxiety, or mental health problems and you start to hear yucky, belittling, degrading, or hate-filled voices, or multiple voices telling you to do different things that aren't in your best interest, or if the voices confuse you, please consult a professional therapist.

Receiving in psychic hearing is meant to be a pleasant, informative way to help you enjoy your earth life better. It is a method of gathering information from other layers and levels, with the goal that you will take this information and be better able to do your work, be in relationship, raise your family, and progress on your path of soul growth. It is *never* scary, belittling, or negative.

Exercise: The Voice Within

This exercise requires you to get out of the house and out of your routine—to hit the road, so to speak. It also requires a little record keeping, in a journal.

For the next three days, you'll be noticing all the ways in which the Divine is communicating with you in psychic hearing, via voice, sound, and word. Once you start paying attention, you may be shocked at how much information is coming your way.

Before you start, set intention for this exercise, so the Divine knows what you need help understanding. Take a minute and write down a question you'd like the Universe to answer for you. Skip the obvious questions like "What are the winning lottery numbers for this week?" The Divine has much bigger fish to fry for you! Instead, select a really useful, important, heart-opening, soul-searching question, such as:

- Does the relationship I'm currently in represent the highest possibility for me? What soul lesson are we to complete together?
- Am I doing my life's work? If not, what is it?
- Am I to travel? Explore something new? Where? Why? When?
- How's my health? What areas do I need to pay attention to? Who can help me in this process?

  1. Pick one of the sample questions above, or create your own. Again, work on only *one* question at a time, so the information is easy to interpret.

2. Write the question down in a journal or someplace you can refer to it.

3. Now, go into meditation or prayer, and request that the Divine provide information to you on your question, using sound, voice, word, or sign. Say thank you in advance! Then go about your day.

Here comes the fun part! Take your notebook and write down clairaudient information that comes your way. You'll be amazed how frequently the Divine is helping to direct and guide you. For example, say your question was about travel. Here's how it might go:

1. Soon after writing down your question, "Will I travel? Where? With whom?" you head out the door to grab a coffee and do some errands.

2. While at Starbucks, you overhear the woman in front of you talking about her recent trip to Austria. "Austria!" you think, "I was hoping for Australia." But you write it down anyway.

3. When you get back in the car, you flip on the radio, and sure enough "Edelweiss" from *The Sound of Music* is playing on your normal alternative rock station! WTH? But you make a note of it.

4. On a whim, you drive by a local travel agency, and sure enough, "Vienna packages on sale now!" is on their signboard.

5. Finally, nearly overwhelmed with all things "Österreich," you mention it to a friend—and she immediately squeals in surprise, "I've always wanted to go to Austria! Can I come with you?"

You get the picture. If you pay attention, and keep track, you will find that the information you receive in psychic hearing—in sound, voice, word, and sign—is very, very clear.

This voice, that voice. Do not be overly concerned, who owns
which voice. In these vibrations, all is Divine.
We speak the same tongue.

—The Messages

eight

Seeing

The entire Universe may be revealed to you in visual reference;
it is the simplest task for you to see this way.
—The Messages

Clairvoyance, as psychic seeing is often called, isn't any big thing. Yet it's often the one skill that gives students the most trouble. Why? It's certainly not because it's harder to "see" clairvoyantly than it is to "hear" clairaudiently. The skill level is the same. In fact, for many people, clairvoyance is actually the easiest technique to master.

Now, before we go any further, let's make sure we synchronize our vocabulary. So, what is clairvoyance, exactly? Officially, it's this:

Clairvoyance (psychic seeing) is the ability to see images in your mind's eye, or as a vision, beyond all boundaries of time and space. This imagery, often embedded with symbolic or emotional meaning, allows you to explore the present and envision the future.

The idea of seeing things can get a little tricky for some folks. Sometimes, this translates into fear.

After all, nobody really minds if an angel or saint has a few words of advice to give us. We're all so used to hearing our own thoughts in our head, in our mind's ear, that eavesdropping on a Divine voice seems pretty small potatoes.

But this idea of "seeing things" in our mind or "having visions" is more intense, isn't it? I mean, what if we actually do see angels, spirit guides, and so forth, in physically palpable ways? What if real-life angels with actual wings start showing up in our living room? This kind of visioning surely is a paradigm shift.

Or, what if we have a vision of something unpleasant; what if we see information about our lives or our future that we really don't want to know about, such as the fact that we'll get divorced, or someone we love will get sick or even die? For these reasons, psychic seeing can be hard for people to wrap their minds around.

All good from good

Getting antsy at the idea of psychic seeing? Here are a few things to remember.

First off, the Divine's on your side. Their purpose in working with you is to assist you in the process of your soul growth. They are here to provide comfort, guidance, support, and to bestow love, bliss, and transcendence upon you. No harm can ever come to you with this connection.

Second, in this book and in my practice, I work only with the Divine. I do not work with any lower energies or entities that might be roaming around. I don't have any time or space for that. I have very clear boundaries around this. Thus, any exercise in this book is pre-set in a Divine container; only good things will come your way.

Third, the Divine works to your comfort level. Your guides are well aware of what you can and can't process, and they respect your wishes for how fast—or slow—you want to go. In fact, if anything starts to move too fast for you, you can simply ask the Divine to please slow down, and they will accommodate you immediately. You can absolutely trust, relax, and let go of any fears that you might have about Divine seeing.

How does psychic seeing work?

Disclaimers completed, let's talk about what psychic seeing looks like. In general, you're going to see in your mind's eye. Some people like to talk about viewing screens, or seeing with your third eye, and I use these terms myself. But of course, there is no actual viewing screen floating around in front of your forehead. Your human body does not actually contain a third eye. These are just terms that help us pay attention, so we can work more effectively.

Most psychic viewing happens in your mind's eye; the first time you try it, you may be surprised how easy it is to do. That's because seeing in your mind's eye is extremely similar to how you see when you are:

- Dreaming
- Daydreaming
- Meditating
- Visualizing
- Imagining

You do these things all the time with ease, day and night! The difference is, with dreaming, daydreaming, and meditation, the images flash though your mind at random—often so quickly and so bizarrely, you aren't able to track them, or make any sense of what you are seeing. However, when we work in psychic seeing, we can slow the speed of information way down, making it simple to examine, explore, and make sense of what we are seeing.

Three ways of psychic seeing

Typically, the images or visions in psychic seeing arrive in three ways:

- As sensation, such as a color, the presence of light/dark, or lights flashing. This type of seeing doesn't provide us with interpretable information, but it does let us know that we're moving from one level of consciousness to another. If you start to receive sensations, don't panic that nothing more is happening. If you stay with these sensations for a while, eventually they'll turn into more useful visual information.

- As an actual image of something that really exists. This could be an object, location, landscape, building, person, piece of clothing, picture, chart—anything that can be physically seen. Sometimes the image is still, like a snapshot, and sometimes it's moving and active, like a movie. For example, you might see an image of a key painted with purple nail polish, and you'll realize it's your house key, which is also painted with purple nail polish. The Divine is showing you a very specific image of something real.

- As a symbolic image, an image of something that means something else. For those of you who have taken classes in literature or art history, this kind of symbolic thinking will come easy. It's what you wrote in all those term papers that began "The shirts in F. Scott Fitzgerald's *The Great Gatsby* symbolize . . ." or "Chagall's use of the color blue in his paintings symbolizes . . ." That kind of thing.

Basically, symbolic imagery is visual information that contains a deeper idea. In the case of psychic seeing, these are usually very simple constructs, sometimes even visual puns. For example, if the Divine was trying to communicate the idea of "empty nest" to you, here's how it might work:

1. In your mind's eye, you might see a nest, with two eggs in it. It might look like a real nest, or it might look like an illustration or cartoon.

2. You notice that the eggs have fallen out of the nest. You might see them fall, as in a movie, or they might just show up on the ground. They're not cracked, just resting easily on the ground.

3. "Oh, it's an empty nest!" you might think in recognition.

4. Upon that realization, you reflect on the fact that your youngest child just headed off to college, and your other child left the year previous—you yourself are experiencing "empty nest" syndrome.

5. You notice again that the eggs, speckled blue and precious, are completely safe and unharmed.

6. You breathe a sigh of relief—your kids are fine, even if you miss them.

7. The "empty nest" image allowed you to address a situation in your own life, and you have reassurance that all is well.

That's how the Divine communicates using symbolic imagery.

Finally, the Divine communicates with imagery embedded with meaning or emotion. As we've learned already from viewing actual or symbolic images, a key isn't always a key. Sometimes it's the key to our house, lost in the sofa.

But it might also be a symbolic key, such as the key to our heart—and when we look a little further, we find an embedded meaning or emotion that is meant to inform and heal us on a deeper level. When you see an image in your mind's eye, whether it is symbolic or actual, always look for this embedded meaning.

Here's an example of an image of a key that contains an embedded meaning:

1. You see a key in your mind's eye, and right away you know it's a symbolic image.

2. You run through all things a key might symbolize: opening, unlocking, being allowed access, etc.

3. You notice the key seems to be vibrating or glowing, as if it wants to tell you more. You suddenly realize that there is an embedded meaning behind the key.

4. Suddenly a heart also appears in your mind's eye. It's a human heart, and its meaning is "love." You don't know how you know this—you just do.

5. You see the key floating toward the heart, unlocking it. You suddenly experience a flooding of emotion, as you realize that the Divine has unlocked your own human heart.

6. A powerful feeling of comfort surges through your body, and the issue that you have struggled with for so long, the closing of your heart, simply dissolves into pure love.

7. You come out of trance, and realize you have been healed.

You may see with your eyes, and you may see with your soul.
We say: open to what Is. Look into the place where all information,
all knowing, all consciousness is contained.
This is where you will truly see.

—The Messages

But can you trust it?

For whatever reason, people find it harder to trust clairvoyance than their other abilities. For example, in workshops, folks see their first visions, open their eyes, and then say:

- How can I trust what I see?
- What if I'm just making it up?
- What if it's my imagination?

My answers, in order, are: You can. You aren't. It's not.

I know that trust takes time. I know that most of you will need to have the experience of psychic seeing over and over again until you can begin to believe in it. I'm all for independent thought and skepticism, rather than everyone leaping over the cliff like lemmings. However . . . I also know from my experience that what you see will be accurate, useful, and correct. So until your own trust starts to build and grow, I'd like to suggest that you accept the possibility that you can trust what you see.

That's all.

In fact, one of the most interesting things about psychic seeing is that you won't be able to see what's not true.

Tom was an experienced spiritual seeker who'd trained at the feet of gurus, teachers, and workshop leaders. He'd traveled the world, attending seminars and retreats. He knew the lingo, the language, the practices, and in fact, I was pretty excited to work with him; I thought because of his extensive background, he'd be able to easily enter psychic seeing, and discover very complete information about his future.

The problem was, what he wanted to see wasn't true.

He wanted to "see" that a particular woman was in love with him.

But she was not.

And because this was not the truth, the visions and images to support this view did not show up for him. The Divine can't—and won't—lie.

Psychic seeing only shows truth. If something is true, you'll easily see pictures, images, movies that tell the story.

If something's not true, you'll see what is true—or you won't see anything.

In the case of this client, as we started to work in psychic seeing, taking a quick glance at neutral situations, everything clicked—he was a great clairvoyant! Then, the questioning turned to this woman, and suddenly he got restless—he was squirming in his seat.

"I see her, I see her," he practically shouted. "She's running to me, she's saying she loves me!"

However, my own psychic seeing of the situation was very different. I almost always see what a client is seeing during a session, and this time I saw vivid images of the woman putting up a wall to keep him away, shaking her head "no." At one point, she even put up a stop sign!

Every visual message that came to me showed clearly that his love was one-sided—she did not return it at all.

As I asked him to explain more clearly what he was seeing, his agitation increased. "She says she loves me," he said vehemently, and then "I can't see anything, I don't know why I can't see." And then . . . "It's all gone black. There's nothing there."

At this time, my own guides said quietly to me, "He has seen the truth."

In the next moment, my client went silent, and I could sense the great sadness of the embedded emotional meaning pervading his heart. At last, he fully understood that this woman was not his love, but a fantasy, and that his heart was broken and in need of healing. He sobbed in the chair across from me.

Not knowing what else to do, I held the connection to the Divine open, and opened my own heart in compassion. Soon the room filled with a pale, golden light, and I soaked this Divine energy in, praying that my client might be able to do the same. We sat this way, as he cried, until his crying was done.

Sometimes, when the truth seems to be more than we can bear, we'll do anything to block it. For this client, experiencing psychic seeing of the truth seemed unbearable—until the Divine stepped in, and not only showed him the truth in a gentle way but also provided the heart healing he needed.

Each of us has walked in similar shoes. Each of us has been disappointed, has had our heart broken. This session in psychic seeing was a gentle reminder that we are all progressing at our own pace, in our own way, and the Divine never presses us to go faster or further than we are able.

An example of psychic seeing

Remember also that when you're seeing something in your mind's eye, you can always ask to see more. You can ask to shift directions or perspective, get closer, view from further away, and so forth, including:

- Zoom in and out, the way you can with a camera lens
- View 360 degrees
- View from all perspectives
- Go from room to room, the same as a "guided tour" on a computer
- "Click for more info" or ask for a deeper level of information

You're in control, and if you aren't seeing clearly, simply ask to be provided with a new view or further information. The Divine will instantly comply.

For those of you who still aren't quite ready to dip your toes in the water without just a little bit more direction, here's an example set out chronologically, so it's easy to break down how it works:

1. A male client comes to me for a reading. His main question is about a relationship he has just ended, with a married woman.

2. Closing my eyes, I see a movie of the woman in my head, with children around her; I ask the client if the woman has children, and he says yes.

3. My client reveals that this woman nearly got divorced to be with him, but at the end, decided to stay married.

4. I see the children doing all kinds of healthy, fun children things: riding bikes, eating popsicles; it's almost a stereotype, how wholesome these images are! I take this to mean the children are healthy and happy, and the woman has made this choice for her children, and that it is a correct choice. As I think this, I see the woman's face in my head, and she is beaming with happiness.

5. I next see an image of my client, with a "poof" of relief over his head, like a cartoon bubble. I feel the embedded emotion of relief. He's suffering now, but for some reason, I know his pain is nearly done.

6. I tell the client that he will be over this woman soon, and he nods his head. "I loved her, but I knew it wasn't meant to be," he admits. "I could feel that things needed to end."

7. As he's talking, I notice another person coming into view. The first thing I see are the feet: a kind of earth shoes, and unshaven legs—I see the unshaven legs first, because I'm supposed to notice them. The word *bohemian* flashes in my head. This is a new woman, and I see a giant heart pulsing in her chest. She's perfect for him—relaxed, unconventional, a whole new kind of woman for this man. I see them at a café eating, and I notice the weather and the foliage around them says "summer." He's laughing, and I can see his heart in his chest, fully expanded in love.

8. I check into the longevity of the relationship, and I see a road that extends endlessly in the distance. In my mind's ear, I hear, "They have as long as they want together" from a guide, who is beaming with joy.

9. After the session is complete, my client and I recap what he's learned, and felt, and experienced. He walks out feeling positive about the future to come.

As you can see from the above reading, I started with psychic seeing, but as other information began to arrive, I used that, too. Usually, readings are a collage of different techniques and tools, and together they mix to provide the most complete truth of the situation.

Exercise: Seeing What Is

I'd like you to experience a way of psychic seeing that allows you to see symbolically, and also experience an embedded meaning. For this, we'll practice with a blind reading, just to keep everyone on his or her toes! Because you know you can't influence the reading in any way, you're even more impressed by what your psychic seeing reveals.

1. Do your setup, as described on page 13.

2. Create some images in your mind's eye. This will look and feel like you're just "imagining" it, or "pretending" or "daydreaming," and this is fine! It's all the same to your brain! Picture each of these images in your brain, and after you picture each, go ahead and erase it with a big imaginary eraser, before you imagine the next one:
   - A bluebird
     (Now erase it.)
   - A plate of scrambled eggs with melted cheese on top
     (Now erase it, etc.)
   - A dandelion
   - A child's toy truck

- The letter *K*, capitalized, in blue
- The number 3, in green

3. Getting the hang of it? Now, in this same, daydreamy state of mind, go ahead and allow any imagery, visions, dream, movies, or any kind of visual information whatsoever to pop or float or dance into your mind. At first, you might just see a color. Wonderful!

4. Ask the color to "tell you more" or "show you more." And notice what other imagery starts to float in your head. Remember, it might be actual, or symbolic, or symbolic with emotional meaning embedded.

5. When an image comes along in your head, don't judge it. For now, simply put aside the comment "Oh, that's my imagination. I'm so weird; that's why I'm seeing a giant blue genie!"

6. Allow the visual information to expand and unfold. You may see actual images, of things you recognize, or symbolic images. Or you may see symbolic images embedded with emotional meaning. In this case, hold the symbolic image in your head—for example, let's say the blue genie presents you with a dazzling green gem—your next step would be to ask for the meaning behind the green gem. You may be flooded with information and emotional understanding about that, which the Divine wishes to impart to you.

7. When you've felt like you've seen enough, count yourself out of trance, open your eyes, and return to this reality.

8. Go to page 241 to see the question this blind reading answered for you.

9. Spend time journaling or thinking about how it all worked—that even though you didn't know the question, you nevertheless answered it perfectly.

In our communications with you, we utilize the simplest imagery,
so that you will understand our meaning.
When we create image for you,
we also create a meaning behind the image,
so that you receive full understanding.

—The Messages

Part Three

—❦—

Direct Connection

nine

Guides & Angels

There is no time we are not with you! Merely say the word,
and you will feel our presence, receive our love, and understand
the guidance that we have for you. There is no time you are alone.
—The Messages

By now, your intuition is becoming attuned. You're learning to sense energy; spot signs, synchronicities, and strands; and hear and see what's happening around you on a cosmic level. This is tremendous progress!

But the best news is . . . there's more.

Because while you've been entering other layers and levels and gathering the info that's there, many of you have also begun to notice something else. On the periphery of your awareness, you may have noticed the presence of other entities.

You may have, while receiving clairaudiently, heard a new voice, and wanted to listen more closely. You may have, while receiving clairvoyantly, sensed that a being or entity hovered at your side. You may have sensed a crowding of energy densities surrounding you, or filling the room. You certainly have felt an emotional surge or flooding, such as the presence of love, or bliss, or grace—but you may not have understood where—or who—it came from.

You have become aware of these energy presences, because you're ready to take the next step along the intuitive path.

In this chapter, we're going to delve deeper, and experience one of the most fun, rewarding, comforting, and beautiful aspects of intuition—meeting and working with your spirit guides and angels.

The ascended, the saints, the Holy Ones:
these are as vast as when they walked this earth.
Their work continues beyond time and space, as it has forever.
—The Messages

You are not alone

You are not alone in this Universe. In fact, as you work through this chapter, you'll come to understand that this Universe is a pretty crowded place! Guides and angels and other entities abound, especially once you know how to see and hear them.

In fact, my first introduction to the intuitive path was via spirit guides. I tell this story in detail in my book *Writing the Divine*, but for those of you who may not have heard it, here's the gist:

In the spring of 2004, a spirit guide knocked on my front door—and then, he floated through it! At the time, I'd never heard of spirit guides, and in fact I didn't even believe in them. Funny, how our belief systems change with experience! But believe in him or not, there he was—a slight, bald man wearing a kind of baggy clothing, which I would later identify as an Indian dhoti or something very similar.

Think Gandhi without the glasses.

People always ask at this point what he looked like, and what they mean is, how did I see him? How did he appear to me? The best way I can explain it is that he did not have the same *energy density* that you and I have to each other; he was not as solid.

They also ask how I felt—was I scared? Unnerved? Excited? All I can say is that this was an extraordinarily intense experience, one of the most intense of my life, but for some reason I wasn't afraid.

He seemed so very familiar.

When you meet your own spirit guides, you'll also find this to be true. They are so very familiar—as if you've known them since you were a baby, or in a previous life, or in every lifetime you've ever had. Because in fact, you have known them that long.

Forever.

Always.

Beyond life, death, time, and space.

Now, some people have angels instead of or in addition to spirit guides. Or saints, or holy beings, or Jesus, or Kwan Yin. Or a spirit animal. Or some kind of combination animal/person entity.

Does it matter who shows up for you? No, it does not. Why do some people have some kinds of guides, while others have completely different types? I have no idea.

Each of us will communicate with an absolutely unique mix of entities, with some of the "biggies" (Jesus, Kwan Yin, etc.) coming up for many people. However, in general, the guides you might expect to see may include:

Spirit guides

These entities usually look fairly human: they dress in clothes, talk with accents, have physical characteristics that you notice, have funny hairstyles, that kind of thing. They may be any age—wise and timeless, very young (childlike), or as ancient as some gnarly old ancestor. One of my clients has a leprechaun! They may laugh, joke, use slang, scold you like your old granny, and so forth. But don't be fooled! These beings may appear human, or more human than the other guides, but they are so far ascended and elevated from where we are that it boggles the mind.

I once asked one of my own guides, Hajam, why he was always joking around with me, always so funny and cheerful. To which he responded, "Because you hear me better that way." I realized immediately how true this was: my personality responds much faster to silliness and humor than to dry solemnity.

Your guides will work with your personality, too.

Our guides don't actually exist in physical "form" as we humans do. They have a different vibration that is beyond earthly form. Instead, they create what we see: the image that appears to us. Being efficient, they do this in a form that we can assimilate and respond to best. You wouldn't frown at a baby if you were trying to get his attention. No, you'd smile, laugh, and coo—this is what babies like!

To our guides, we're pretty much babes in the woods. That's one reason they often act like buddies or trusted friends—because that's a way we find it easiest to understand what they're saying. Of course, many people's guides are serious and stoic—it all depends on your personality and what kind of approach is going to catch your attention best. Funny or serious, don't be fooled: all guides are sublime in their power and gifts—as holy as any of the holy beings you will encounter.

Angels

Angels are the Divine messengers you read about in the holy texts of most religions. There are angels in Africa, Asia, Australia, Europe, and North and South America; I'm sure there are even angels in Antarctica! One interesting thing about angels is that they may or may not have visible wings. For example, when I received *The 33 Lessons*, one of the entities who arrived was Archangel Gabriel—but he did not arrive as a seven-foot angel with giant wings. Instead, he arrived as a gentle teenage boy with curly hair, and I didn't see any wings at all. There's been plenty said about guardian angels, other kinds of angels, angels from the Bible, and so on; if you're deeply attracted to angels, you probably already know plenty. Key archangels and angels are common guides for people to have—they're grand communicators, and they make a point of communicating with many of us! If you don't know much about angels, don't worry; you'll know what they are when they arrive, wings unfurled or not.

Ascended teachers

These are master teachers who don't present as comfortably "human" as your everyday spirit guides. You will know these beings because they are usually tall and wear robes. (I don't what the deal is with the robes and biblical outfitting—it must be that this method of dress is easy for us to perceive, so that's how they appear. It's as if all the ascended masters got together and said, "They expect robes, so let's give 'em robes!") They are often older, such as the wise ancient being with white hair or a long white beard. However, they may appear in many other ways, too.

Saints and holy beings

Saints and holy beings often include well-known departed and living presences who are known for their impact on humanity, such as Mother Teresa, the Dalai Lama, Jesus, Buddha, Kwan Yin, Joan of Arc—beings and entities from all kinds of cultures and belief systems show up under this category.

Other guides

These may appear as more mystical, magical, unidentifiable, and possibly from other dimensions. These aren't the same as aliens, which are beings from other planets that live in a current or concurrent reality. Instead, these are beings from other layers and levels of dimension. It's not difficult to recognize this sort of being; they don't look like what you've seen before. For example, one of my clients has a dazzlingly beautiful guide who has a brilliant jewel in the middle of her forehead, right at the third eye. Not something you see every day at the mall!

How it all works

We'll talk about how to communicate clearly with your spirit guides soon, so relax for a sec. I can tell that some of you are getting very excited about this possibility, maybe even holding your breath! One, two, three—exhale! This is exciting, but bear with me now as we talk about how it all works.

Knowing what to expect, as opposed to the various rumors and untruths and misconceptions that are so vividly portrayed in movies about guides, angels, and entities, can make all the difference between a successful experience and one that's confusing and unclear.

First, you may *see* them—or you may sense them. It doesn't matter which happens. "Thinking" you see them and "sensing" you see them is that same thing, energetically. Again, for emphasis: *seeing* and/or *sensing* is the same thing, when it comes to spirit guides and other Divine entities. The faster you can accept this, the further you can move forward.

You may *see* them in the room. You may *sense* them in the room. You may *see* them in your mind's eye. You may *sense* them in your mind's eye. It's all the same thing. Now, of course, on TV shows they film it differently, with liberal use of smoke machines and flashbacks and so on, but in reality, the intuitive realm is very subtle. It is not necessary for you to see things in the physical flesh, in physical dimension, in the same vibrational density as your own body, for them to be absolutely, 100 percent real in the etheric realm.

Sensing, seeing in the mind's eye, hearing in the mind's ear or with telepathy—these are all ways that spirit guides and angels communicate with us. In very highly charged circumstances, such as matters of life and death, or times when we absolutely need assistance such as a near-death experience, they may appear more earthly or flesh-based. But for most of us, most of the time, this is the exception—not the rule.

Personal-help hotline

When you need help, angels take charge, causing immediate and direct Divine interference. Nothing soft or smooshy about these Divine messengers! A few years ago I was driving home from Seattle to Salem, about a four-hour drive. It was late afternoon, rush hour, and the highway traffic was crazy busy. I was exhausted, distracted, and unnerved by the intensity of the traffic, and just wanted to get home. Suddenly a car cut in front of me! I had no time to react, and even as I saw my car veer toward the back of the car in front of me, I felt it swerve out of the way. I didn't have time to react—my hands didn't turn the wheel; my feet didn't work the gas or brake. And yet, my car swerved, almost as if someone else had taken control of the wheel. Which, of course, they had.

I felt the adrenaline flood my body—you know, the way energy screams down your thighs and your stomach feels sick? I knew I'd narrowly escaped a severe, perhaps even fatal accident. In a flash, I noticed an angel riding on the hood of the car, on the driver's side. He was full-winged, wearing a warrior-style breastplate, and he was fierce. He turned and nodded to me, then resumed his post. My heart brimmed with gratitude, as I realized he was here to protect me on this long trip home.

Nowadays, I experience this kind of support on a continual basis. I'm 100 percent certain that this is happening for you, too, if you stop to recognize this! Look around, as you circulate in your day. Watch for those who appear more elevated, joyous, loving, dazzling. There is a good chance these beings are angels, of one kind or another.

Exercise: Divine Reunions

You've been in the path of spirit guides and angels your entire life. But now, with this exercise, you're going to begin to sense, hear, and see them. There's a lot to learn with these guys (and gals), so take your time, and repeat these exercises as needed.

I'll use the term *spirit guides* for this entire exercise. You may see angels, or holy beings, or something else entirely. No worries; whatever arrives to you is just fine—it's just terminology.

Finally, the "three-level" concept and Spiritualist methodology for this and the next three exercises were shared with me by my colleague Reverend Drew Vogt, an extraordinary Spiritualist medium in San Francisco (find him at http://sites.google.com/site/revdrewnew/). Thank you, Drew.

1. Do your setup, as you did on page 13.

2. Now, imagine that you are going to take a step up in vibrational level. Your body will stay where it is, but your consciousness

will take rise onto a step or platform that we'll call level one, the vibrational level of peace and tranquility. Take the step now. Notice how the air around your skin seems to shift—does it seem to shimmer or tingle? Notice how your heart seems to open— does it feel expanded? Experience how this feels.

3. Now, we're going to take a step up to level two. Imagine yourself taking this step, and picture what this new step or platform looks like. It might be a simple white step, or an ancient stone slab. You decide what it looks like. This is the level of love and light. Step up to it now.

4. Imagine you have a small gauge to discern how much love you are feeling right at this moment. Look at this gauge. Is it at 30 percent? 150 percent? 3 percent? Don't judge where you are. Just be with wherever your love gauge registers.

5. Now, bring attention to your heart area, and imagine that your heart is cracking open, painlessly and beautifully, to let some Divine light in. Feel how great it feels to be opening to this Divine healing light. You may feel your heart begin to expand in your chest, in a wonderful, beautiful way.

6. Next, we're going to move up to level three. This is the level where you can meet your spirit guides and angels most easily. Later on, we'll use this level to meet the departed, but this time, we're using it only to meet your spirit guides—that's it. We're setting that boundary for this exercise, so that only spirit guides can show up—no departed are invited to this party!

7. As you step onto level three, you'll sense, see, or notice a congregation of spirit people in the distance. Take a moment and notice these beings—sense them, see them, imagine them.

8. Now, ask the particular spirit guides who will be working with you for this session to step to the right, in a smaller cluster. Watch as they start walking or even dancing over! Most folks will have two to eight guides in this cluster to the right.

9. After your cluster has formed, ask the particular guides who are working with you today to come and step into three positions: (a) behind you, (b) to the left of you, and (c) to the right of you. Don't worry too much about who moves where—they know what to do!

10. Take a moment to sense each guide, in each position: to your left, behind you, to your right. Occasionally, there will be two guides in a position.

11. Ask one of the guides to come stand in front of you, and notice which guide moves into this position. Again, don't worry; they know what they're doing!

12. This guide will have something to say to you, either telepathically or in words. Chances are 100 percent that you will understand the message completely, at some level.

13. When this guide has finished, ask if another wants to come forward. If so, see what this guide has to tell you.

14. After you've heard from two or three guides, it's time to take a break. This is challenging, new, and intensive work! A little goes a long way when it comes to the Divine.

15. Walk yourself down to level two, the level of love and light, and notice how your love gauge is registering now—if you were at a 3 percent earlier, you may notice you're at a 300 percent. Or not. Don't judge, just notice.

16. Walk yourself down to level one, the level of peace and tranquility. Relax here.

17. Walk yourself into your earth reality. Slowly count back from ten and open your eyes. Notice how everything looks brighter?

18. If you feel like journaling, write down what you experienced when you met your guides. If you don't want to journal yet, just relax, and think about what has happened. You may feel overwhelmed, emotional, energized, over the top. Feel how you feel.

What just happened?

Congratulations! You've just met your primary spirit guides and angels! This is a profoundly emotional experience, as if you've just met the people you've loved most and best for your entire life, and your life before that, ad infinitum. Now that you've met them, let's talk about why they take which positions, and what it all means.

Please remember that I teach from my own experience, and from the guidance I receive. If your experience is different, trust your own experience. The Universe is a vast and wondrous place, and there is room for everything and everyone.

That said, here's how the guides tend to arrange themselves:

On your left is your *earth guide*. This guide is the one who helps you with earthly concerns: job, partner, money, health, etc. This guide appears fairly human, and may have a strong personality. This guide has been with you since birth, and in all your previous lives, and will be with you for all your next lives. Pretty awesome, hmmm?

Behind you is what I sometimes call your spiritual teacher, or your *downloader*. I can't tell you how many training sessions I've taught during which clients report that this guide is tall, white-haired, and wearing a robe, like Gandalf in *The Lord of the Rings*! In fact, that's what my own guide looks like who stands in this position! I don't know why there would be so much similarity across a wide spectrum of people, but take it for what it's worth. Other clients have Jesus, Mary, Holy Ones. These are the Big Guns! In any case, this spiritual-teacher guide provides you with Universal knowledge, connects you with collective soul, unified field, Akashic records, etc. Often, this guide will provide what I call a *download*, where your brain opens up, and all the information of the Universe will flow right in. Nice!

The guide to the right is your *protector*, or alternately, your guide of transitioning into other dimensions. Some people have spoken of having lions to the right, or winged angels, or warriors. My own is a mystic woman who protects me as I work in the etheric realms, when I work in mediumship, and when I travel outside of earth reality. This guide takes care of you, helps you transition from one realm to another. Sometimes I think of this as the mystic guide.

These guides to the left, behind, and right are with you for all your lives: past, present, and future. They're your primary guides—a.k.a. your posse. They know your ins and outs, ups and downs, where you are on your path of soul growth. They know everything. Don't even try to lie, or fib, or distract 'em! They're you're peeps, and they're here to help, any day, any time, 24/7. You can't get rid of them, even if you try.

And, what happens if you have an additional, fourth guide in any position? Why, simply ask them what they are there for. In some cases these are specialty guides to help with specific issues in your soul growth.

We are here to translate the ineffable: we offer meaning
for that which is beyond lexicon, beyond comprehension.
We also bring love, which is understood by all, at every level.

—The Messages

ten

More Spirit Guides
& Angels

We are with you as helpers and teachers.
We are with you as guides to other dimensions and
layers you cannot understand fully as humans,
without assistance or translation.

—The Messages

Who exactly are these spirit guides and angels you contacted last chapter, these beings who are now hopping up and down with excitement, a palpable presence at your shoulder, filling the room with glowing light?

Or, maybe it wasn't that clear.

What if you *think* you saw spirit guides—but you're not sure?

Or, what if angels did make themselves known—but it's all kind of hazy?

At this point, I'd like to address the questions of the uncertain, the wary, and the independent thinkers in the crowd—which I'm hoping will be all of you! I'd also like to address the needs of those of you who experienced something—but aren't quite sure what you experienced. Finally, I'd like to speak to those of you who had a totally blissful experience with your guides and angels—and are chomping at the bit to go further!

First off, wherever you are on the spectrum of experience, it's perfect. There's no right place to be at this point of first contact—there's only the place you are. Some of you are moving very quickly, and that's great. Some of you are taking more time—that's exactly what's supposed to happen. Your guides know exactly where you are at this point in your life, and they are helping you to open and awaken at a pace that is most beneficial to you.

Too fast, and it will be disconcerting.

Too slow, and you'll get bored.

Thus, regardless of "what happened" for you, or what didn't, and depending on how deeply you entered the deeply relaxed stage of psychic trance, and how emotionally fulfilling your session with your spirit guides or angels was, I'd expect you to be feeling and thinking something like this:

- It's all in my head.
- I made it up.
- It's my imagination.
- It's that liverwurst sandwich I ate for lunch.
- It's my subconscious.
- It's my higher self.
- I'm nuts!
- The author is nuts!
- I never should have inhaled in 1982.
- It's aliens, for sure.
- I hope my friends don't find out what I'm doing.
- I'm not doing it right.
- I don't think I met any guides or angels; or maybe I did. I'm not sure.

- I couldn't see them clearly—but I think I felt or sensed something.
- I couldn't hear clearly—but I think they were trying to say something.
- This is kind of weird, but it's really interesting.
- I'd like to see if I can go further next time.

On the other hand, for those of you who went very deep and had a lovely guide/angel experience, your thoughts might run along the lines of:

- Wow! I have spirit guides!
- Wow! I have angels!
- Wow! They were so familiar to me, as if I'd already known them!
- They spoke to me telepathically!
- I could hear their words!
- They showed me things clairvoyantly!
- Holy moly, I can't believe what they showed me—that sure makes sense!
- I feel strong, supported, clear, sure, and fantastic.
- I can't wait to meet them again.
- I'm in awe, I feel great, life is good!

And for those of you who had very clear experiences, you might also be thinking:

- I can't believe these guides have been with me all this time!
- I can't believe I never paid attention to them before.
- I can't believe I have this amazing gift of intuition.
- I can't believe I never used it before!
- I'm going to start using this amazing, Divine, super-smart, and super-powerful resource all the time!

As you'll notice, every time you have communication with the Divine, you experience a flooding of emotion, and you feel overwhelmingly great, fantastic, superb, sublime. What's more, every time you have this kind of direct connection with your guides—even if it's hazy or murky at first—the easier it becomes to meet them, communicate with them, and understand the messages they are giving you.

Would you not reach down a hand to a child, the young, the small, the new? In this same way do we reach to help you, to assist you, to provide illumination and heart's healing.

—The Messages

No middleman required

This idea that we can communicate directly with God/Divine/One/All/Source/Universe and understand the cosmos on our own, without a priest, guru, rabbi, or other middleman, is a relatively new concept. Until recently, most people in America went to church to be preached to—in other words, they allowed the priest or pastor or church leader to interpret God's word for them.

The concept that you could understand Divine concepts on your own?

It wasn't there yet.

But people prayed by themselves, you might argue—and yes, that's true. But it was often by rote, and the party line was that when you prayed, you were sending messages, pleas, and petitions up to God, and if you were very, very lucky, He would think about it.

Certainly, you never expected Him to answer! At least not in a direct, two-way conversational kind of way that you could understand! Back then, only rabbis/priests/pastors/deacons/bishops/gurus/shamans/witch doctors were allowed to disseminate Divine teachings. The idea of direct connection was seen as blasphemy, the devil, insanity . . . or all three.

I'm not making judgment on what happened back then.

That's just how it was.

Go back further through the centuries, and you'll find that people were often persecuted or tortured or run out of town or labeled witches for holding any beliefs that differed from that time and culture's accepted thought. Remember the Crusades? Or the thousands of other religious wars this earth has seen?

I'm not making judgment on what happened centuries ago, except it all seems rather bloody and misguided.

We've come a long way since then.

Yet jumping forward from the past, we began to notice a shift in how we think about God, church, and the rest. One of the most recent shifts, a mere blip on the earth's timeline, started in the 1960s and '70s, the decades of free love, tuning in, turning on, and T.M. In this era, people started understanding that they didn't need a priest, pastor, guru, or the like to direct and translate the word of God, or any of the dazzling information lurking in the cosmos.

A middleman was not required.

They could receive it by themselves.

This movement really got going when people like the Beatles and Ram Dass started flocking east in search of their guru. Think of it! A whole generation starting to meditate and do Eastern practices. What a scene!

I'm oversimplifying, of course. But the gist of it is this: over the centuries, we've shifted from church/religion telling us what to believe to the understanding that we can have a direct connection on our own—no gurus, priests, rabbis, or others necessary.

If this were the 1600s in Salem, Massachusetts, you'd have been burnt at the stake. If you were in Europe at the same time, just the thought was punishable by death. Even now, in countless places around the world, and quite definitely in the United States, this kind of thinking is still taboo:

God talking to you?

The Divine in communication with you?

The Universe at your beck and call?

The Universe providing specific information you need?

This kind of thinking is still shunned by many.

Even though the answer to these questions is of course Yes. Yes. Yes. And Yes.

Walk your own path

This direct connection idea? It's what we've evolved to. We are fully able to have direct, two-way communication with the Universe/God/Divine/One/All, as it is brought to us in energy, messages, guides, angels, and myriad other ways, at any time, in any place.

No translator required.

As we look more closely at this, we also see that it isn't just that we don't need priests/rabbis/religious icons for direct connection. We also don't need the spiritual leaders who are so prolific today: workshop leaders, presenters, authors, celebrities.

This is because after a certain amount of exploration working with different practices, teachers, and so forth, you will come to realize that there is no teacher on this planet who can provide you with more than you can get on your own.

After a certain point in your own evolution, you must begin to walk your own path, and begin to discover the answers that await you in your own conversation with the Divine.

No one else has the answer.

No one else knows the secret.

You have to figure it out for yourself.

And you can do this using direct connection.

Infused with the Divine

Every time you practice meeting your spirit guides and angels, you become more connected to the Universe/Divine/All/One. Even if it's just for ten minutes, your energetic vibration is raised. Even one experience of meeting your guides and angels is enough to bring about life-changing transformation.

How does it work? Well, think of the Divine like a giant eyedropper full of food coloring—you choose the color: blue, yellow, red, green. Think of yourself as a glass of water.

Now, add a drop of food coloring to the water, and notice that the color of the water starts to change. One drop, it's just the faintest tinge of color—in fact, maybe it still looks clear. Two drops, you're definitely seeing a light shade of the color, and this color has begun to diffuse rapidly throughout the molecules of the water. By three drops, the water is definitely the color of the food coloring. The more drops you add, the more the water becomes the shade of the more concentrated food coloring. At a certain point, the water becomes fully saturated with color—there's no way for it be more fully blue, yellow, red, or green than it is.

The same is true when you become infused and steeped in the Divine. At first, you're water, and the Divine is food coloring. But after a few drops of Divine infusion, you begin to change; you are no longer just water—you are Divinely infused water! After a while, you become as fully infused with Divine energy as a human being can. At a certain point, you are saturated and filled with Divine, so that there is no difference between you and the Divine.

Enter in to direct connection frequently enough, and just like the water that is fully infused with the food coloring, you become fully infused with the Divine. There is no difference between you and One/All/Universe/Source.

You are the same.

Now, regardless of what you did or didn't experience in the last chapter, this time you're going to experience more. In fact, every time you decide to have a direct connection and work with your guides, you open that window a little wider. You become a little more infused with the Divine. Even if it's infinitesimal for you at the start, take heart! It will happen!

A final word—this isn't the only way to meet your guides and angels. Remember what we just looked at, this idea that you are in charge of your own path, and that all the spiritual teachers and workshops and training in the world can never be more useful to you than your own experience? The method I am presenting to you is one way to walk the path. If, as you close your eyes and start your direct connection, something else entirely begins to happen for you, go with that!

As long as you choose to have your window open, the Divine knows how to reach you in the way that's most profound and meaningful to you.

How your guides help

Your guides are here to help you with literally everything your soul requires in this lifetime, as well as all the other lifetimes you've had or will experience. This means they can help you with the nitty-gritty details of life on Earth, such as:

- Career
- Relationship
- Health
- Location
- Life's path
- Life's purpose
- Your next best step
- Your highest possibility

They can also provide the most interesting, advanced, and amazing information about more etheric aspects, such as:

- Energy
- Metaphysics
- Spirituality
- Time
- Space
- Other dimensions we don't understand
- Other concepts we don't know about
- God/One/All/Universe/Source

People who are extremely adept at receiving this particular etheric kind of metaphysical information often become channels or channeled writers. If you notice you're starting to receive that kind of information, grab a pen and write it down! The information may be valuable for you—or it may be meant for the world.

Symbolic objects

As you spend more time with your guides, you're going to notice that they often want to present you with a gift, such as an object, image, message, or word. You'll receive this by seeing it in your mind's eye, or you'll "just know" it's there. You'll instantly understand the symbolic meaning of this image.

What kind of objects might show up? Well, it could be anything. But in recent client sessions, these are a few of the objects that guides provided:

- An acorn
- A chalkboard
- A vault full of treasures
- A wheelbarrow full of dollar bills
- The word *fear*
- The word *embrace*
- A silver bracelet

Let's take a look at how these objects worked, in terms of revealing a message. First, each of these clients entered in to meet their spirit guides, allowed them to arrange in their positions, and then asked one spirit guide to step in front. In each case, this guide presented them with an object, which the client accepted by taking it into their own hands. This object provided a clear answer to their question.

Harry, a man in his late thirties, asked a question about where his new business was going. His guide gave him an acorn, and Harry immediately thought of the phrase "From an acorn, a mighty oak grows." He said, "When I heard that, I knew that all was well, and that time would build my business." He breathed a sigh of relief that starting small was fine—what was coming in time was big, solid, and stable.

Vida, a woman in her mid-twenties, wanted to know what her life's purpose was. Her guide pulled out a blank chalkboard, and Vida had the immediate flash that it was "a blank slate, waiting to be written on." She understood she could create whatever she wanted, from the multiple ideas she had, and all would be correct. "This makes sense," she told me. "I've been feeling pressured to pick just one thing, and now I see that I don't have to choose. I can do more than one thing at a time."

Robbi, a woman in her early forties, wanted to know about her life's path, and immediately was taken on a journey by her guide to a vault filled with gold and treasures. This was accompanied by the phrase "You can sleep soundly." She understood that all material aspects were taken care of in this life and this was not an area that she had to worry about. She soon began to attract money so easily that she began to be able to support several charities.

Janine, in her mid-forties, had recently lost her job, and she wanted to know what was ahead. Her guide, in very humorous fashion, pushed a wheelbarrow toward her, and she saw that it was filled with cash. With it came the phrase "More than you can spend." She also understood that this would not be immediate, but in the near future—the next few years. With this knowledge, she started her own business (as she'd wanted to do for years) and watched it succeed.

Ray, now thirty-four, wanted to know how to reawaken his psychic abilities, which he'd had as a child, but then shut off for twenty years. He saw the word *fear* written on a piece of paper, and understood that the only thing blocking his abilities was fear. Next, he received another piece of paper, upon which the word *embrace* was written. He understood that he could embrace his psychic abilities. During this particular session, Ray received a profound amount of emotional healing from his guides.

Renee, in her early sixties, was having trouble remembering how to reach her guides. Her guide showed her a silver bracelet, and gave her the idea that she could touch it whenever she wanted to be in contact. "It's so easy," Renee exclaimed in tears, as she came out of session. The next day, she found a silver bracelet similar to what she'd seen, in an antique store. Now, whenever Renee's out in the world and needs a little Divine guidance, she can touch the bracelet. Of course, no bracelet is required. But for Renee, it's a talisman that makes it easier for her.

Exercise: More Divine Reunions

1. Do your setup, as described on page 13.

2. Go up to level three, until you are in the place and space where you notice your spirit guides have gathered.

3. As before, ask the guides who will be working with you for this session to cluster to the right. Then, ask the guides to stand behind you in their proper positions: left, behind, right.

4. In your mind, ask them a specific question that you would like help with. This may be about career, relationship, life's path, life's purpose, and so forth: whatever you have concerns, questions, or need more information about.

5. Notice which spirit guide comes to stand in front of you. Is this your earth guide (from the left), your spiritual teacher (from behind), or your mystic helper (from the right)? Or does an entirely new guide appear for this particular question? Or does something else happen? If it does, trust that this is correct, and simply go with it.

6. Receive the message your guide has to tell you, clairaudiently or telepathically. You will notice that he/she has a gift or object to give you.

7. Receive the object, as well as the flash of symbolic meaning that goes with it.

8. If you have questions about the meaning of this object, ask the guides to help you understand. You may say in your mind, "Tell me more" or "I don't understand. Please show me more clearly." Your guides will provide more information, until they are satisfied you understand the meaning.

9. Be dazzled by how well your guides know you, how perfectly appropriate this object and meaning is for you!

10. Journal or think about what has happened, and what it means to you.

We are not always easy to see, but we are always with you.
When you seek us, look to the spaces of what is unseen.
This is where we reside.

—The Messages

eleven

Advanced Guides
& Angels

*When you connect with us, you connect with all that is seen, unseen,
holy, Divine. We are merely conduits for All/Universe/One.*
—The Messages

So, what happened this time? How do you feel? What did you experience? Are you starting to understand the way it looks, sounds, and feels when you're in contact with your guides and angels? How simple it is to work with them, and how the information is provided to you clearly, in ways that you can understand? How your vibrational level changes and shifts, each time you seek a direct connection with the Divine and enter in to the etheric realms? How you yourself become able to understand things on a deeper, cosmic level that's beyond intellect—one that reaches right into the core of your heart, and allows you to shift and heal in ways that you haven't been able to before?

Yes! Double yes! This has either happened for you already, or is beginning to happen now. As we've discussed before, everyone is unique in how they progress in their awakening or opening. You may feel you're just beginning, while others may be further along. No worries. Just keep practicing and entering in, and before you know it, it will begin happening for you.

Enough times entering in, and pretty soon you'll be telling me that you're experiencing bliss and transcendence and hanging out at a state of higher vibration—not just while in you're in formal meditation or trance, but all of the time. You'll also notice that all those supposed problems you once faced in your life are starting to dissolve, deconstruct, and disappear—right before your eyes. That's because:

- A little bit of Divine infusion goes a long way.
- A little bit of Divine infusion is more than enough to transform your life.
- The more you enter in to the layers and levels of consciousness where it is easy to infuse yourself with the Divine, the more you raise your vibration.
- The more your raise your vibration, the happier you will be.
- The happier you are, the easier and faster you can create a life you love.

No wonder the Divine's been the feel-good secret of the ages!

In this chapter, we'll journey yet another step into the realm of guides and angels, and answer some common questions about what can happen when you go further.

One caveat to intrepid explorers: even though we're taking it slow and working in a safe and steady manner, the truth is—this pathway isn't particularly predictable. Yes, it's guided; yes, it's Divine. But I'll be the first to admit that I cannot tell you exactly what is going to happen during your first, second, or three-thousandth session with your guides and angels. Your experience will broadly follow what we discuss here. But as you expand and practice and delve and discover on your own? As you step deeper and deeper into the mystery? Well, the Universe is a pretty big place, and mystical things that you and I don't understand are happening every single minute. In fact, they're happening to multitudes of people on this planet right now—and quite possibly one of those people is you!

However, I can guarantee that the more you practice these techniques, the more quickly those everyday feelings of malaise and ennui will disappear from your life. You know, those low-vibration feelings of:

- Disappointment
- Anxiety
- Indecision
- Despair
- Hopelessness
- Fear
- Anger

Yep. All those negative feelings, doozies for most of us, will start to disappear from your mind, and from your life.

Again, every time you enter in to meet with your guides and angels, you become infused with the Divine. Almost immediately, you will notice that you are starting to shift, that a lot of things you thought you needed (anxiety, fear, anger) begin to drop away, and the person who existed last week no longer exists this week—a new person is in the process of being formed into existence.

The new you may not be fully here yet—but he or she is on the way.

Avoiding the T.M.I. syndrome

Sometimes, when people start working with their guides and angels, they get so excited about what's happening to them that they forget that the nature of this information is deeply private. The guidance you receive from your guides is classified information—it's the kind of deep stuff you might share with a close friend or mentor, or just hold quietly in your hearts.

However, it's not particularly the kind of information you'd:

- Post on Facebook
- Blog about

• Mention in every third sentence of your conversation, along the lines of "My guides told me this . . ." or "My guides said . . ."

It's private. You know.

As in, for your benefit only.

I add this caution here, because in my line of work I know a lot of people in touch with their guides and angels. It's a lovely mystic tribe, and I'm grateful to be a part of it. However . . . sometimes we spiritual seekers get overly excited. We forget that our psychic/spiritual journey is not about getting spiritual gold stars for overachievement. For example, I sometimes hear things like:

"My guides insist I wear purple," or

"My angels told me to quit my job and live in India," or

"My guides said I was Mary Magdalene in a past life," or

"My guides said that I was a Master Teacher."

Now, maybe the above is true . . . who am I to say? But, in general, if you find yourself announcing, "My guides said" to everyone around you, please tread carefully. No one can get better, more accurate, or more meaningful information from your guides and angels than you can—even if you're just starting to learn how.

The information they present is for the lesson you are learning at the moment—once you've learned this lesson, you're ready to move to the next lesson and get help on that.

You're not meant to get stuck, in one static idea, forever.

You're meant to receive frequently, as you learn and grow throughout this lifetime.

For example, a guide may advise you to "wear purple" to a specific meeting, or even for a period of time. But at some point that guidance won't hold true anymore.

It's a process.

Your guides would like you to check in frequently.

They have new information for you, all the time.

You're not required to "wear purple" your entire life, unless of course every time you enter in and receive new information from your guides, they tell you same thing.

In most cases, the guidance you receive will be for a specific situation in a specific time frame. And after you learn that lesson, you'll be ready to work on a new, entirely different lesson. So, go ahead—learn the lessons as they come. Then look to the new lessons as they arrive.

We are always learning and growing.

Leggo your ego

There are lots of gifted, wonderful, compassionate intuitives out there, and they can provide you with extremely valuable readings. However, there are also those who are nothing more than glorified ego massagers, happy to sit there boosting you up to delirious heights, for the price of a reading.

Please, trust your own guidance. If an intuitive tells you something strange or that you don't understand or that seems too good to be true, check in with your guides on your own. I would especially check in on ego-inflating predictions such as:

- "You'll win the next round of *American Idol*," or
- "You were Cleopatra in a past life," or
- "You'll write a bestselling novel and make millions," or
- "You'll marry a billionaire."

These may be true. But they also feel a bit pumped up, a bit designed to appeal to your ego or your fantasy. I'd like it much more if your reader said something along the lines of:

- "You'll get a promotion at your job."
- "You were a peasant woman in a past life," or
- "You'll write a book that won't sell that well, but you'll learn a lot writing it," or
- "You will marry a kind man with a steady job."

We are not all former Cleopatras. We will not all make millions. We will not all write books that top the bestseller list. We will not all be on national TV. Some of us will—of course! But many of us are meant to live simple and lovely lives in full relationship with our family and friends, and this is the highest, most blessed path we can walk right now.

If you're hearing platitudes, such as those on the previous page, from so-called "experts," check in with your guides yourself, in direct connection. Trust your own guidance, always.

And . . . if you are meeting spirit guides and angels, and for some reason do not feel deeply touched, overwhelmed with gratitude and awe, go deeper. Open your heart further. Ask for the barriers, superstitions, power trips, and ego games to be lifted away. The Divine is profound. Allow yourself to feel it, fully. Even (and especially) if you know this will change your life forever.

The bliss of the Universe is your birthright; it is the core of what you are. Come to us, connect with what is Divine/One/All. We infuse you again and again with this vibration.

—The Messages

Embedded emotional meanings

Do you recall how in the last chapter, your guides provided you with an object, and this object held a symbolic meaning? In addition to this symbolic meaning, your guides are also able create a deeper embedded emotional meaning that contains profound information.

How does this happen? Well, remember your guides don't exist in the form that you perceive them. Who knows what they really are, at their core. A floating mist, a beam of light, a pure color?

In one training session, my client Sandra met four guides, and when I asked her to describe them to me, she told me she couldn't see anything except four pure colors: orange, green, gold, and blue. The guides stayed as pure color for most of the session, even though they were able to communicate with her easily. (To maintain confidentiality, all the names and identifying details of my clients have been changed in this book, by the way.)

It was a good reminder that the guides create themselves and the imagery that we see and hear. They themselves don't actually have appearance or form. They also don't speak English, Spanish, Chinese, or whatever language you speak—they are beyond words and language. They work with us in familiar ways because that's how it's easiest for us to understand them. Once we've gotten to the first stage of communication, they work progressively more in depth. This usually progresses as:

- Simple words and images that clue us in
- Symbolic words and images that help us understand more
- Embedded emotional meanings that provide a complete "knowing" or understanding, and include profound layers of information and healing

Embedded emotional meaning isn't difficult to experience—the guides are hoping you want to receive this. Some simple ways to make it happen are to:

- Ask them.
- Have them touch their forehead to your forehead.
- Create a cord between your heart and theirs.
- Reach out to hold their "hand."
- Accept a gift or object from them, which will contain the embedded emotional meaning.

What you will feel next is hard to describe until you experience it. The best I can tell you is that it's sort of like a giant "whoosh" of energy, in which you understand everything on an emotional and spiritual level, all at once. This "whoosh" can be overwhelming, profound, blissful, or all of these at once. You may feel energy coursing through or flooding your body or brain in an entirely new way, and you may have sensations of being:

- Supported
- Enlivened
- Lifted up

- Healed
- Comforted
- Loved

This energetic or emotional surge is how your guides communicate the embedded emotional meaning of whatever guidance you are seeking. This feeling can be mind-blowing!

Remember: most of us don't experience vibrational energy of this level at any other time in our lives. Revel in it. And know that this sort of Divine infusion can be provided to you again and again.

Downloads—one step further

Sometimes your guides may have an intensive amount of information or energy that they would like to provide to you. You will receive this as what I term a *download*.

If a download is about to happen to you, you'll have the sense that a guide has something to say to you, and you'll know that this is a huge amount of information—much more than can be easily provided in earth time. It's also way more than can be provided with embedded emotional meaning. In a download, the guides will compress the information (think of compressed computer files) so that large amounts of information can be transferred quickly, in a matter of seconds.

Downloads may contain:

- Activation of abilities, such as the facilitation of a psychic opening
- Spiritual teachings
- Metaphysical information that is too complicated for us to receive any other way
- Vibrational raising or shifting
- Scientific or technological information
- Transcendence
- Healing
- And more!

The guidance that I have received about downloads is that they are a method of providing us with information that we need, but that's too complicated for us to understand. One way to think about it—a download is like getting a bit of collective soul, or Akashic record, or cosmic consciousness, placed right into our brain and body, all at once.

In my own experience of downloads, I feel a rushing sensation, like a cascading of energy as a channel or tube from the top of my head (crown chakra) through my whole body. It's either that my body has opened up as a tube, or that my body has become immersed in a field of energy. I see information, such as mathematical and scientific equations. I also receive imagery, color, emotion, and feeling, as well as words, writing, and musical notes. I don't understand what it all means, but I find that after these downloads I understand things more quickly, especially metaphysical concepts. Almost as though they've downloaded the "answer," so that when I have the "question" later in my writing or teaching, it's there for me to use.

Clients have reported seeing different things during downloads. In one recent workshop session, each person in the class received a download at the very same time! All the guides were in the room; all the participants were in deep meditation; and suddenly a massive group download began. This was an amazing experience, and I knew right then and there that part of my purpose was to facilitate this process to more and more people. The Divine is upgrading us!

Each download is different, but the common characteristics are they are good, right, effortless—almost like something you've forgotten has been provided to you again. They are also fast—in most sessions when downloads happen, they're over within a few minutes. You may have a feeling of timelessness or being beyond time as it happens, so a one-minute download may feel as if it's lasting an hour.

If your guide tells you that they'd like to offer a download, by all means accept. Remember: you are only working in the highest level of the Divine. Only good, light, and love comes from this.

Journeys

Often you'll be communicating with a guide or angel, and he or she will suddenly take you gently by your elbow and you will understand that you are being taken on a journey. A door may appear, or a window, or a tunnel, or any other manner of transportation. Time may appear to be moving very slowly, or very quickly, or both at the same time. You may sense you're passing through Universes, or energy fields.

On one recent journey, my client Jonathan said that his body had started to buzz very loudly, almost like an airplane engine revving. Because I had entered in with him during the session, I could also experience this—although in earth reality, he was still sitting calmly in his chair. Next, he felt himself going very fast through some kind of pattern of tunnels—almost like a tube at a water park! He journeyed this way with his guide taking him though realm after realm, until finally he was able to meet his father, who had passed twenty-eight years earlier. Jonathan's father was regal, glowing, and whole, and Jonathan burst into tears with joy at seeing him.

After the session, Jonathan emailed to tell me that this particular journey happened to him three times over the following week, always at night when he was drifting off to sleep. For now, the journeys have stopped. However, I foresee that Jonathan will be soon be taken on other interesting journeys—the more you experience, the more you are able to experience, as your vibration becomes more attuned to the levels of the Divine.

Healings

Your guides and angels will often arrive when you are in a relaxed mood, such as right before you drift into sleep or when you awaken in the middle of the night, and perform a healing on you. My guides inform me that this kind of work is done to make it easier for us to receive and understand—it helps us keep our vibration high. Remember how we raised our vibrational level in order to meet our spirit guides and angels?

The more we can raise our vibration, the easier our life on Earth flows. Healings help us stay in this frequency.

My client Marsha experienced a healing while sitting in her car directly after our session, reorienting herself after the intensity of the session. "I suddenly felt myself drifting into sleep, and I remember thinking that it was fortunate I hadn't started driving yet," she explained. "I didn't pass out—nothing like that at all. I just felt the sweetest longing to rest, and I gave in to it. I don't know how long I sat there—it felt like hours—but angels appeared all around me. They poured a golden honey all over my body, and my body absorbed it. I felt healed, refreshed, and that all was well. When I came out of it, I was bright and alert! The street seemed to be almost shining, the light was so bright!"

If you find yourself receiving a healing, just relax. You may feel that someone is working on you, or notice parts of your body tingling, roaring, buzzing, or humming. You may even have the experience of a psychic surgery—such as an angel or entity energetically cutting, removing, and suturing some organ or body part that may have been bothering you. It's a wild, amazing, almost unbelievable sensation to have this happen—and yet if it happens to you, you will have a fierce knowing that you were in fact healed.

Exercise: Divine Downloads and More

1. Do your setup.

2. Step up to where your guides and angels gather.

3. Ask your guides to stand behind you in their customary positions: left, behind, right, with any additional guides to the right.

4. Ask the guides if they have anything to show you or tell you. If they present an object, such as they did in the last exercise, accept it. This time, after you feel you understand the symbolic meaning, also ask them to show you the embedded emotional meaning. Sometimes, they may put their forehead to yours, or touch your shoulder, or you will see their heart space extending to yours.

5. You will experience a flash or flood of emotion as you are provided with the profound embedded emotional meaning of this word or object.

6. If you think your guides would like to offer a download, journey, or healing, simply allow it to happen.

7. Be in awe of the love, light, and healing you have been provided with, and thank your guides and angels when this session is complete. After this session, write your experience in a journal.

8. Pay close attention to dreams, and other experiences that may take place in the next few days. These often follow intensive experiences with the guides.

All information, all emotion, all healing.
This is what we provide to you in every connection,
in every moment your window is open. Come to us,
again and again. In this way, you become infused.

—The Messages

---

twelve

✿

Mediumship: Connecting with the Departed

There is always communication between souls. Even in death, this ability does not depart. Love tethers us each to other, beyond time and space.
—The Messages

You already know how to work with spirit guides and angels, and communicate with them in higher layers and levels of etheric information. Now, you're going to learn *mediumship*, or how to connect with the departed. Yep. That's right. The departed. You might also dub 'em:

- Ghosts
- Spirits or spirit people
- Those who've gone before

- Those who've crossed over
- Ancestors

Sometimes when we work in this particular layer or level, we might also come across other energies roaming around time and space, which we'll discuss a bit later. These might include:

- Random departed
- Random unattached energies
- Old thought patterns and beliefs, such as fear, superstition, etc.

There's a reason I've waited until this far in the book to introduce mediumship, and that's because successful mediumship has everything to do with vibration. As you've been working through this book, you've been raising your vibration with each new skill. At first, you gathered what you could receive with your senses, eyes, ears. Then, as you did the more complex exercises, you were able to receive more complicated imagery, meaning, and emotion. Most recently, you learned how to contact spirit guides and angels. With each new level of complexity, you raise your vibration even higher.

With this next step into mediumship, we're going to keep our vibration high—although truth be told, mediumship actually uses a lower vibration than communicating with spirit guides and angels! That's because we're going to enter in to mediumship, through the door of spirit guides and angels, at a higher vibration than we actually need.

Why? Well, we could choose to enter in to mediumship using the direct route—by matching the level of vibration of the departed. That's the method you often see on TV or in movies, when gnarly ghosts start flying around the room!

However, if you're looking for a safe, pleasant, and Divine experience with the departed, there is another way.

In order to avoid complications when working with the departed, it's important that (a) you work in the highest vibration you can command. That means choosing to enter in at a higher level than you actually need. You'll also (b) want to make sure you're accompanied by your guides and angels, who will help you hold this level of highest vibration.

By doing this, we enter in to the realm of mediumship with full support of a whole posse of Divine beings.

Simply put, it's the smart way to do it.

Are you ready for this?

With all that said, here's another idea. If you don't think you're ready for this chapter, just skip it. Really. You don't have to learn mediumship. It's not required. You can still explore all your other psychic skills—this chapter is purely optional coursework.

Or, if you feel you might one day want to learn mediumship, but don't feel ready for it right now—then do this part later. Really. You can move along to all the other sections, just fine. I've positioned this section here now, because so many of you will be chomping at the bit, ready to learn this next sequential skill.

But if you want to wait, no problem.

Sounds like a lot of heeds and warnings, doesn't it?

I'm taking this chapter on mediumship slowly, because working with the departed is the one aspect of psychic training that often brings up fear for us. I myself was a big mediumship scaredy cat. Even after my psychic abilities opened in all other ways, even after I'd worked with thousands of people doing readings and psychic training, it took me a long, long time to work up the courage to explore mediumship. Basically, I was afraid of what I thought mediumship would involve: ghosts, hauntings, wraith-like evil spirits, bats (okay, I'm still afraid of bats), demons, and dead people watching me in the shower—all that Halloweeny-type stuff.

But after a certain point, after enough time when I was tired of hearing myself say to folks, "I don't do mediumship," I began to look at my fear.

And to my surprise, I realized that I wasn't afraid because of any scary experiences that I'd actually had in the past. In fact, when I looked back at my life, I saw that I'd already had numerous beautiful experiences with the departed, from the time I was a child.

Instead, I was afraid because *I'd been told I should be*. As children, we're continually bombarded with the cautionary tale. Part of this is to protect us, I suppose, from the yucky stuff that does roam the world. When we give our kids warnings such as "Don't go into the forest" or "Don't walk home by yourself," we do teach them to avoid unsavory places.

And yet.

Even though I was a big scaredy cat, I was also deeply unafraid. I'd lived in Europe for part of my childhood, and the sense of the ancient was palpable in every church we visited, every castle we ever toured. The departed were there in droves, and I could feel them around me—even if I didn't have the words to express what I was sensing. During the time I lived in Norway as a kid, we stayed in a house that had been part of the Nazi resistance—there were underground tunnels that connected to neighboring houses, which had been used to transport persecuted Jews to safe locations. As you can imagine, the vibration in the house was pretty strong! Standing where the tunnels were boarded up, I could sense the people who'd once been there—I could sense their stories, and the fear and panic that permeated everything.

A few doors down from this house there was an old cemetery, where I played for hours. It sounds creepy, but it was a lovely spot; I always felt a sense of peace there, and was comforted by the presence of the departed around me.

Still later, as an adult, I had multiple mystical experiences with my departed father. These are some of the nicest memories of my life. And so, with these remembrances richly filling my heart, when I finally did decide to take on the mantle of mediumship, I released the fear. I remembered the Divine. And as I ventured on to this next fork in the intuitive path, I understood that no matter which realm we inhabit—living, departed, or etheric—all is Divine. There is yet again no separation.

Better dead than alive?

Still a tad nervous? Don't be.

For the most part, the departed—even those who were rotten rapscallions while living—are improved versions of their former selves.

Something about the new reality they find themselves in agrees with them—they're lighter, more expanded, more aware. Heck, they're existing in a new, Divine state of consciousness! All of their past anger, guilt, bad behavior? They don't have that anymore—or at least not very much of it. They've either incarnated to a new life already, or are doing some Divine reflecting and processing of their own. Plus, they're actively mentored by spirit guides and angels, who work with them the same way they work with you, only even more directly.

In other words, they've been rehabbed!

Mostly, the departed are wiser, kinder entities who are happy doing whatever it is they're doing. They may be curious about you, and they'll like it if you acknowledge them. But mostly, they're just doing their thing. Sometimes, if they're people you know, and if it's the first time you've made contact, they'll have something to tell you. Sometimes, you won't know them at all, and they'll still want to stop by, say hello, tell their stories. For example:

- The land where I live is etherically populated with tribal peoples who once settled along the Willamette River in Oregon. I sense them frequently; they often watch me from a distance. Almost any time that I step outside, I will notice that they are standing or sitting quietly amongst the trees or at the edge of the meadow. They aren't harmful or ominous in any way. They just are.

- A few entities live closer to our house. There's the man on the mound, as I call him, who always wears a plaid shirt and an old hunter's hat. There's also the girl in the upstairs bedroom, about age seven, who has also appeared to my youngest daughter. These spirit entities don't want anything from my family or me. They're just here, working on their stuff. I used to find it uncomfortable when I became aware of them, but now I simply acknowledge their presence, and let them be.

- At my office in Portland, which was formerly a gardening center, I'm often greeted by an older spirit couple—they're nearly identical farm folk, dressed in chambray work shirts, overalls, clunky boots. I always allow them to stay (but not participate) in the sessions I do with folks here, and they usually hover near the ceiling, appreciative of and interested in the goings-on. Frequently, they clap or laugh, or tell me they enjoy the work I am doing!

These beings, which represent just the tiniest fraction of all who exist, inhabit a different layer or level of time/space/consciousness than we do, yet they inhabit it just the same. How many layers, how many levels are there, replete with etheric beings of all kinds? Ain't that the question—how many angels on the head of a pin?

If you wish to speak with the departed, do so.
We say: they await your communication, even now.
Even now, they delight in you.
—The Messages

How you'll see 'em

The departed will appear in the same general way as spirit guides and angels—you'll sense their presence, or see them in your mind's eye. Some people do see them as fully formed entities: not quite human in their density, but pretty close. If this happens to you, no need to be alarmed; just let it happen.

Whether you see or sense, you'll often be able to tell what the departed are wearing—what their hair color is, facial features, other physical characteristics. As with any aspect of clairvoyance or psychic seeing, don't worry too much if you see the departed in your mind's eye, or if you just sense their presence. Just start with where you are, and don't worry too much about if you're "doing it right." You are.

I personally get a little freaked out if I start seeing the departed in too strong of a physical form; I actually prefer to see them in my mind's eye, so I request to see them this way. It's silly, I know—like closing your eyes and pretending the other person can't see you! If you want to see them only in your mind's eye, just ask them to appear that way.

Spirit animals

Even though I'm a bit shy around departed people, I'm very comfortable seeing departed animals in a strongly physical form. In truth, I've had some of the most eerie and mystic experiences of seeing spirit wildlife appear unexpectedly—one second they're there, fully formed and glorious, and then the next, they're gone. A young deer walking out from the mist, so close that I could have placed my hand on her back. A giant black dog, appearing from nowhere on the country road I walked, racing faster than it's possible for a dog to run. One minute these spirit animals are there, sweating, breathing, their scent filling my nose; the next, they've simply vanished. Instantaneously and utterly gone.

These may be totems or spirit animals, or they may be animals that are departed, or departed persons who create themselves as animals. For example, I am frequently visited by my departed father, who creates his presence as an enormous bald eagle. I have seen that eagle in some of the most unusual places—on an overpass to an urban highway, on a stubby pine tree on Christmas morning—places where you don't normally see eagles! In all cases, spirit animals are marvelous to behold—they will literally take your breath away, and their emotional meaning or message is usually quite clear.

Bring in a bouncer

When you work with the departed at the highest vibration, you'll also be working with one of your spirit guides. This guide is often the guide who stands to your right. (If it's not, don't worry—your guides know who's who, and who's supposed to be doing what!)

As you work in mediumship, this particular guide will act as master of ceremonies or as a bouncer to your experience—he or she will direct which departed communicates with you first, and for how long. If you always have a guide serving as your MC or bouncer, your experience is always going to be pleasant, easy, and enjoyable. In fact, my best advice to you as you work in mediumship is: never enter in without a guide.

You wouldn't attempt to climb Mt. Everest without a Sherpa, would you?

You wouldn't explore the Lost Caves of Mystery without a guide who knows them inside and out, would you?

You wouldn't eat *torafugu* (poisonous blowfish) without the chef who'd prepared it standing by, would you?

Of course you wouldn't. And, for these same reasons, you're not going to enter in to meet and greet the departed without a guide right beside you—running the show, keeping the riffraff out, and protecting you at every moment.

Crowd control

A little fair warning? After your first communication with the departed (such as after you've done the exercise in this chapter), you may wake up the next day to a surprise—a crowd of departed on your ceiling, all waiting to talk to you! Or, you may be out at the grocery store, and suddenly sense multiple presences who'd like a little attention. Or at home in your living room, you'll suddenly know that there are a bunch of 'em hanging out in the room, hoping you might have time to chat.

You might know them. Or you might not. Oddly enough, these departed may have nothing to do with you! They're what I call random departed, spirit folks who have somehow discovered that your particular window is open, and like it or not, they'd like some attention now, please.

You may find that these random entities arrive in full force, like shoppers to a Black Friday sale, the minute they know your window is open! For example, the day after I had my first experience with the departed during which my father and grandmothers showed up, I woke up the next day, eager to do some more work with my deceased relatives. That's when I noticed the aforementioned crowd of random departed hovering on the ceiling, filling up the space in the room—they were even hovering outside of the house, waiting to come in!

Being a curious person, I decided I'd call in my guides and take a look at who these departed were, and what they wanted. I experienced, in order:

- An old-time cowboy, dusty from the range, who told me he had a problem with his neck. When I asked him what the problem was, he said that he'd broken it falling off a horse. "Are you sure you weren't hanged?" I asked, noting the thick rope around his neck. Sheepishly, he drawled, "I guess I was," and then proceeded to tell me in gory detail about how he'd been hanged, from what tree, and so forth. "Am I related to you, or do you have a message for me?" I asked. "No ma'am," he said, hanging his head. He'd just seen my *window* was open, and wanted to tell his story.

- A diminutive European woman from World War II, who wore a militaristic type of suit or uniform. Was she German? She was thinking about her husband, who had died earlier; not in the war, but from a disease. She told me he had a heart problem. "Do I know you?" I asked. She didn't answer; she just kept talking about her husband.

- A slender young American lady, who was dressed 1940s style. She wore a skirt, blouse, cardigan, and a knotted scarf at her neck. She was crossing the street to mail a letter. She told me the letter was important; it was to a lover she was missing. "He's coming for me soon," she said, but I had the strong feeling he was not.

- A Buddhist monk in ancient robes; he looked as though he came from thousands of years ago. He was young, maybe fifteen or sixteen, and mischievous. I couldn't understand his words, but then he telepathically told me something to the effect of "I just showed up because I can," and then he laughed.

By this time, I was starting to get a little tired and confused—how come these departed didn't seem to know me? How come I didn't know them? How come none of them had anything relevant to say? I was beginning to feel I'd entered some kind of psychic ice cream shop with a take-a-number machine. "Next." "Next." "Next."

I plowed diligently through about seven more of these random departed, and then I saw the line wasn't getting shorter—it was getting longer! They were arriving, faster than I could keep up. I conferred with my guide, who was standing in amusement by my side, waiting for me to figure it out.

"They're not going to stop coming, are they?"

"Nope."

"I could sit here all day, couldn't I?"

"Yep."

"They aren't important to me, to my life's path, or to anything I need to know about? They're just random departed, who've found my window open, right?"

"Correct."

"Uh, can you make them go away?"

"It's up to you."

With that, I took one last look at the line of departed snaking from here to eternity, and closed up shop for the day. It was easy—I simply requested that my guide gently send them all away, which he did instantly, with a twinkle in his eye. It was a good lesson, and I'm glad I learned it early—otherwise I'd probably still be stuck in that room, listening to the plights of every single random departed who wanted me to hear what he/she had to say!

If you find yourself being bombarded by random departed, simply tell them nicely that you can't help them. Explain that you only work with those who have a message for you, or something meaningful to tell you. If you get really stuck, ask your guide to work as a bouncer! Almost instantaneously, the departed will disappear from your field of recognition. Above all, don't worry that if you don't visit with every departed who shows up, you'll miss out on some VIP or spirit celeb. You won't. If there's a departed you're supposed to talk to, your guides will make sure you do.

The yuck factor

It's true. There are yucky entities in the Universe. It's also true that one of the goals and intents of this book is for you to avoid them! As I've said ad infinitum already, the best way to avoid yucky entities is to connect with your spirit guides and angels first and let them act as bouncers, if need be. They can do this . . . and they will.

My own experiences with yucky entities have ranged from no-big-deal to mildly unpleasant, and my hope is that your experiences will be equally manageable. If you work through your guides, at the highest vibration you can muster, nothing will be too bothersome. A few examples of what I've experienced lately:

- In a recent session, I worked with my client's departed uncle. This spirit was tormented, sad, miserable. He revealed a great deal of suppressed information about my client's family—abuse, mental instability, addiction, you name it, this family had it! Hearing this was a great relief to my client—she'd always sensed it was there, but the truth had been hidden for generations. During this session, two of my guides were fully present and directed everything. However, that night before I fell asleep, this particular departed spirit reappeared to me and tried to get me to communicate with him. I felt vulnerable because I was so tired, and immediately called upon my guides to help. With my Divine bouncers by my side, I announced to the departed that I'd already done the work to completion, and I wouldn't be available to him again. He left immediately. I have not heard from him since.

- In another session, a young girl appeared in the room, alternating between playing happily and standing sadly near the shoulder of my client, a woman in her fifties. The girl's sadness was palpable—I felt it in every pore of my body. When I asked my client who the spirit girl might be, she told me that she'd had a younger sister who'd died at age five. The departed confirmed that she was indeed the sister, and I felt her emotions even more fully. She was sad, she told me, because she worried about the sister she'd left behind. Almost as soon as she explained this, the mood lifted and I felt a sunshiny, butterfly sort of happiness fill the room. The spirit girl told me that while moments of sadness still came, she was happy knowing her sister was okay and she was content in the etheric realm, where she still played as a child.

Possessions, hauntings, and so forth

Sometimes, the departed get so wrapped up in a place or a person, they can't seem to leave. My clients sometimes tell me about yucky entities in their homes, or they themselves sometimes might feel yucky—as if an entity is so close to them that they can't remember themselves anymore. This sounds terrifying, but it doesn't have to be. Just as in real life, it's all about setting boundaries.

If you think of unwanted entities as bums and bullies, or even just as tricksters or mischief makers, you're on the right track. If you understand that your own high vibration, when combined with the high vibration of your guides, can get rid of any problematic characters, you're really on the right track.

If you find yourself attracting entities you don't want around, ask yourself why. Is your vibration too low? Are you forgetting to have a guide accompany you? Are you working without proper boundaries?

For example, a young woman came to me because she was being pestered by the departed day and night. There were there when she opened her eyes in the morning, staring her in the face! They even showed up at work, hanging out in her cubicle. Obviously, this woman was a gifted medium! As we talked further, it turned out that this spirit-following had been going on since childhood, and at this point, my client was sick and tired of it—she wanted these spirits to go away!

"They never leave me alone," she cried with worry. "They follow me everywhere."

"Do you talk to them?" I asked, curious.

"Oh, I'd never talk to them!" she said incredulously. "I try to pretend they're not there."

"You ignore them?" I asked her again. It just didn't make sense. Suddenly, I felt a little energetic nudge at my elbow, and it all became clear.

"Say . . . do you have a guide with you when you see these spirit people?" I asked casually.

"A guide?" she said, blinking her eyes in surprise. "What's a guide?"

As it turned out, this extremely gifted medium had been seeing the departed all her life—yet she'd never risen to the higher vibration where her guides, angels, and other Divine entities gathered. As if she'd been in the foothills all her life, and had never seen the view from the mountains.

Of course, this woman had all the power she needed to rid herself of unwanted spirit folks—she just didn't know it yet. Because her mediumship had started when she was just three, she'd always believed that the departed were in control, that she was at their beck and call. From her childhood, her only defense had been to ignore them and pretend they weren't there. Somehow, in all those years of being a medium, even into adulthood, she'd never considered there was another option.

In our session, I had her enter in and meet her guides and angels. She was afraid, but bravely went forward, and was stunned when she felt the Divine love and bliss of her guides and angels.

"I've never felt like this before," she said in awe, as she rose in consciousness and awareness. That simple shift in vibration did the trick—along with my explaining to her that she was free to set boundaries around spirit people at any time, and her guides would provide complete support at all time.

In earth life, you determine whom you want to be involved with, and how much time you want to spend with them. These same boundaries also apply to entities. If they show up uninvited, it's your right to simply show them the door. Usually, a direct statement such as "You are not allowed here" or "I am not available to you" or "Go away" is all that it takes. If you need bigger guns, call in your guides, request their help, and watch as they do the dirty work for you.

Above all, don't be scared. You're stronger, tougher, and more powerful than any departed, because your vibration is higher. As long as you remain in high vibration, you'll enjoy encounters with the departed that are filled with love, light, and healing.

Exercise: Beyond the Veil

As we enter in to work with the departed, remember that we're going to set an energetic boundary of Divine Access Only. Remember also, as with everything you've experienced while working on the exercises in this book, the experience you will have now will be easy, light, and love-filled.

1. Do your setup.

2. As before, follow the guidelines from chapter 9 for meeting your spirit guides and angels. This time, add that you would like to open your window to any departed who are relevant to you.

3. Ask a guide to step forward, to act as a bouncer or master of ceremonies for this session.

4. You will have already noticed or will soon notice the energies of the departed in the room. They may be on the ceiling, very near you, in any part of the room. Ask your guide to allow the departed you will be communicating with first to step forward.

5. Notice who the departed is, and see if you can identify them. For example, it may be your paternal grandmother—but she may look different from when you knew her. For example, she may present as a young girl, not a "grandma" type.

6. Ask the departed what he/she would like to tell you. Usually, you will understand this telepathically. If the departed has an object to give you, accept it, and also ask for the deeper embedded emotional meaning of the message.

7. If there are things to be cleared up or set right with the departed, now's the time! You can speak to them telepathically, and vice versa, or in any of the ways you've received information from guides.

8. Your guide will tell the departed when "visiting hours" are up. This is important, as often the departed are so happy to have found a window open that they'll act like the proverbial neighbor over the picket fence, sawing your ear off with anecdotes about this and that. If after a while you feel like the departed is just try-

ing to prolong their stay, just tell them that time is almost up—
and watch them get to the point of their message, fast!

9. Sometimes, entire family clusters will show up in multiples; this
   is fine. If they are all talking at once and you can't understand
   them, ask your guide to tell them to communicate in a more
   orderly fashion.

10. If at any time things start to slide sideways, get weird, or feel
    uncomfortable to you in any way, simply call upon your guide,
    who will instantly correct the situation for you. No worries.

11. After visits from a few departed, you'll find yourself getting tired
    and needing a break—you'll be at your limit for this session.
    Stop before you become too exhausted. Don't try to press further
    or see "how many you can do." Remember: they'll be there next
    time!

12. When you are ready to be finished with this session, step down in
    vibration back to present reality, and open your eyes.

13. Do something earthy, grounded, and easy for the rest of the day:
    have lunch, take a shower, pick up your kids from school, watch
    a movie, walk the dog. Enjoy yourself as an earth being, living an
    earth life.

Only the physical body dies; the soul exists beyond time.
In this way, communication is always possible,
from one soul to another. Recall this
in times when you yearn for those who have departed.

—The Messages

Part Four

Relationships

thirteen

Healing Relationships

*Healing is an act of intention; it is the calling forth of love into present
reality. This manifestation is yours to use in endless supply.*
—The Messages

Let's take a moment to check in and see where you are on this part of
your journey along the intuitive path. As you already know, whenever
you enter in to the etheric realms, such as when you practice clairvoyance, clairaudience, sense energy, communicate with spirit guides, and
so on, you become infused with the highest vibration. Furthermore,
when you become infused with this vibration, something else begins to
happen—you start to become *transformed* by this energy.

At this point in your journey, it's very likely that you're seeing the
results of this amazing shift in your daily life in very tangible ways,
such as:

- Your relationships are starting to get better.
- You're becoming clear about your life's path.

- You're beginning to trust in the Divine—even if it doesn't make sense.

- You're starting to let go of anger, pain, and fear.

- You notice yourself filled with love and light more often than before.

- The Divine has become a constant source of connection and support for you.

- You understand that love is our highest vibration.

Hmmm. Seems like in a mere twelve or so exercises of entering in for Divine infusion, somebody just got a PhD in metaphysics! Go ahead—pat yourself on the back for allowing yourself to explore, experience, and move forward as a Divine being in human body. Then, after you've finished floating around on an energetic cloud nine, please drift back down to earth, and plant your feet squarely on terra firma.

Hate to tell you, but there's quite a bit more work to be done on the intuitive path. And this time, the work we're going to tackle is more challenging than any we've done up to this point.

It's harder, it's trickier, and it's more humbling.

That's because it deals with . . . relationships.

Relationship matters

I work with lots of different types of clients: folks of all ages, creeds, backgrounds, from all over the United States and even across the globe. You'd think with all of this diversity, people's issues and concerns would also be diverse.

But it's not so.

In fact, what I've found is that whether you're from Austin or Auckland, Seattle or Sydney, the majority of people have one shared concern that affects them all. There's one big thing that comes up in every single session, every single time.

Wanna guess what it is?

Well, it's not money, material "stuff," or success, although of course those are always hot topics. It's not health, career, or what city to relocate to. It's not even loftier things, such as life's purpose or life's path. Instead, what people want to know most about is relationship. Especially, they want to know about:

- Spouses, partners, and romantic relationships
- Family relationships, including all the many variations we have nowadays with blended families
- Friends and acquaintances
- Colleagues, mentors, and teachers
- Enemies, rivals, and nemeses

The money, "stuff," success, and so forth—it pales in comparison. What's top of mind, what affects people the most deeply, always concerns relationship: who we love, who doesn't love us back, who we don't love, who loves us anyway.

Of course, a client might start a session with questions about income stream or health concerns. But when you get right down to it, after enough peeling of the proverbial onion, relationship is what matters. And what may surprise you is that this doesn't just include our relationships to those who are living. It also includes our relationships both to those who have departed—and to those who are yet to be born.

Can't we all just get along?

Even after millennia of human experience on this planet, we still haven't learned how to play nice with any degree of consistency. Oh, sure, we've learned to love some people some of the time: spouses, kids, parents, friends. But this idea of opening our hearts to folks who aren't in our immediate tribe? Well, it can be a doozy.

It's not that it's difficult to experience the sensation or the energy of love. As you know by now from all your work in higher vibration, it's pretty easy to get the love vibe going. In fact, I can't tell you how many workshops I've taught where the vibration rises up past the roofline, and sure enough—hearts bust open, tears roll, bliss happens, and pretty soon that room full of strangers becomes a room full of the nicest people you could ever know; there's a love glow coming off every single participant!

At one workshop in Seattle, for example, the room was radiating with energy so strong we could see it—we were literally drenched in luminous glow. During a break, I went out to grab some food with some of the participants, and realized we looked like addled love zombies to the rest of the world: we couldn't stop laughing, our eyes were crinkled in smiles, we were fully open to each other! Everybody else around us seemed energetically flat compared to our wonderful, blissed-out vibration. It was a great feeling—a complete rush—and this high vibration, this love vibe, is how we're meant to live with each other, all the time.

Life in the bliss zone is awesome—but it ain't easy to sustain.

At least, that's what I've experienced in my own life, and observed with my clients. Even when people are fully conscious, evolved, and actively working on their "stuff," relationship difficulties arise. Consider these client examples:

- A woman in her late fifties wants to be closer to her ailing dad, who's near ninety. But because of a fight they had thirty years ago, he refuses to take her phone calls.

- A grandmother won't stop sending candy to her daughter's kids—she says it's her right as a grandma. The daughter throws the candy away, while the kids wail in disappointment. Everyone's upset with everyone else.

- In the spring, an adult brother and sister argue over who gets which furniture from an elderly parent's home. By winter, they are no longer speaking to each other.

- A couple divorces after twenty-two years of acrimonious marriage, and then spends the next ten years bitterly fighting over the (now adult) children.

- Twenty-five-year business partners have an argument over a deal. They can't come to an agreement and end up suing each other.

Three ways to heal

It's easy to say, "Big deal," "Get over it," or "Suck it up" when you're looking at these relationships from a place of detachment—i.e., when it's not happening to you. But when you're right there in the fray—when you're the daughter, the sister, the colleague—then emotions get fired up, feelings get hurt, the unwinnable game of "who's right" comes into play, and it's very hard to see the forest for the trees.

We fight and argue and have miscommunications with each other, because we are human beings. We're conscious to a certain level—and then, unfortunately, that's as far as we can get. We can reach the higher vibrations; we can attain the love vibe; we can understand with our hearts and minds that we are all One: no different, no separation. Yet even understanding this, we still get upset with each other.

Sigh.

We find it hard to crack open our hearts. We find it hard to take off our emotional "armor." We're afraid. We're angry. We're uncertain. We don't trust. And sometimes, like a cut that's never cleaned, a simple misunderstanding between us can fester. Sure, it hurts to pull off the scab and disinfect the wound. But if it goes on too long, it can scar badly, never healing as it should.

Healing relationships with intuition

The good news is, no matter how impossible it seems right now, you can heal the relationships with those you love—and even with those you don't love very much at all! Best of all, healing these relationships does not have to involve a lot of uncomfortable, emotionally sticky scenarios that make people resist making up in the first place!

Instead, you can use three handy intuitive techniques that will amaze you with (a) their simplicity and (b) their effectiveness. These are:

- Healing relationships through soul-to-soul communication
- Healing relationships with energetic cords
- Healing relationships through vibrational alignment

Remember what we've talked about—that you don't always need to know exactly how things work in this realm for them to work really well? Well, this is one of those cases. Put your quantum-physics calculators down and let your left-brain mind relax as you read on and learn more. Then give the exercises a try—and see for yourself.

> *You may choose to move along quickly in your soul growth, or more slowly. This is the choice of each soul.*
>
> —The Messages

Healing via soul-to-soul communication

First, any relationship issue can be resolved simply, easily, without emotional pain, and so quickly that you may perceive it as being miraculous!

How? By using direct telepathy to communicate with another, soul to soul.

It's not hard, but before you start, you'll need to accept two concepts. I say "accept" them, because of course you already know them. Once again, it's all about trust. These helpful factoids are:

- Regardless of how much you are currently bothered by the person-of-issue, the particular human being you are currently waging emotional warfare with is actually a soul in a human body, just like you.

- Regardless of how much you are currently miffed by him/her, you are in fact both Divine beings in earthly containers.

See, that's not so hard!

Now for the really cool part: when you are using telepathy as a tool for healing, you can completely avoid dealing with the bothersome earthly, human person that's making you tear your hair out. Instead, you can work directly through the Divine, on a soul level.

This means you can bypass the human, cranky personality with all its ego, jealousy, and drama, and instead communicate energetically—

soul to soul. In fact, you can work soul to soul with any other person, even with groups of people, as easily as you've done any other exercise in this book.

I know, I know.

It all sounds so "woo woo."

And yet, with my clients and in my own relationships, I have seen soul-to-soul communication work unfailingly and instantaneously. It works, because it's based on the same methodologies that we use anytime we working in Divine vibration.

When you communicate soul to soul, you set things in motion on a Divine level. As you already know by now, the Divine can do quite a bit more extensive work than we, ego-laden humans, can. If you've got a big relationship problem to solve, why not let your Divine posse ride on over and help you out?

How does it work?

Basically, you enter in and raise your vibration to the level where you can communicate with your guides. Then, accompanied by a guide, you invite the soul of the person you wish to resolve things with. Then, the three of you—you, your guide, and the other person—have a soul meeting.

Sometimes, people report seeing themselves sitting at a conference table, with the person in question on one side, and a guide sitting near. Sometimes, the other person stands in front of you, while the guide stands to the side. Sometimes, you'll simply sense the consciousness of the other person looming into your awareness. The nicest thing is, this other person doesn't arrive all angry and belligerent (as they may be in real life)—they arrive as a soul: pure, loving, blissed out, and vibrating at the highest level.

Next, you communicate soul to soul—you simply allow your soul to speak to this other soul, with a guide standing by to help. You say your piece. The other soul says his or her piece. Often, this will involve symbolic or embedded emotional messaging. This communication is often astonishingly clear, and may present options you'd never considered.

Working soul to soul

Let's say you're getting divorced. You've gone 'round and 'round with your ex on how to divvy your property up, but no dice. He won't agree to anything. So, you enter in, call up some guides to help you, and you dial him up, soul to soul, and have this conversation:

Your soul: I'd like to talk to you about our divorce settlement.

Other person's soul: [Silence].

Your soul: I'd like to ask that we proceed in harmony, so that we can both arrive at a settlement that satisfies us most. I've offered to split things in half, but you continually reject this offer. Why?

Other person's soul: [Shows you an image of a wedding picture being torn in half, then a picture of a heart being torn in half].

Your soul: I'm sorry that this is causing you so much pain. It's causing me pain, too. I'd like to move forward in harmony, so we don't cause each other any more pain.

Other person's soul: [Shows a picture of a house. Sends telepathic message of "I want the house." Sends emotional message of neediness].

Your soul: Why you didn't tell me you wanted the house?

Other person's soul: [Sends an emotion that feels like guilt or embarrassment].

Suddenly, your guide hands you an object—it's a divorce settlement, all tallied up and ready for you to sign. As soon as you take it, you feel an embedded emotion similar to overwhelming relief, and realize the proceedings will move effortlessly after this.

The next day you go to your attorney and draft a deal so that your ex receives the house, and you get everything else. To your amazement, when the totals are tallied—the property, the savings, the IRAs—the values are equal. Your ex signs immediately, and you divorce amicably.

Or, say you're having trouble with an acquaintance. She's texting you at an obsessive level, and when you don't respond, she texts more! Before you confront her in person, you decide to take a deeper look. You enter in, call up your guides, bring her soul into your consciousness, and have this conversation:

Your soul: I consider us acquaintances, not close friends. I feel uncomfortable having so much contact with you.

Her soul: [Hangs head, embarrassed. Sends message of sadness and loneliness].

Your soul: I'm sorry you're sad.

Her soul: [Sends message of a car accident, and the emotional message of trauma. You suddenly see clairvoyantly and have a deep knowing that she recently lost someone very close to her in a car accident, and she's is in a process of deep grief. She hasn't been acting herself lately].

Your soul: I'm sorry about your loss.

Her soul: [An emotional message of grief, and also gratitude that someone has recognized it].

Your guide steps forward and places his hand on her heart, and you see a column of white light flow to her chest and fill her whole body from head to toe.

In the next days, she doesn't text or message. But a few days later, she does, and you find yourself responding in a new way: detached, compassionate, loving. After a few texts back and forth, surprisingly, she stops messaging completely.

A month later, she sees you at a coffee shop and comes over to say thank you. "You were one of the few people who was kind to me during a really difficult time in my life," she reveals. "Everyone else thought I was nuts."

Why soul-to-soul communication works

With soul-to-soul communication, you connect deeply, at a level beyond argument and ego. Because you are working from a place of highest vibration, you connect in love to each other.

You don't have to forgive—but you may feel inclined to.

You don't have to forget all the terrible things this person did to you—but they may drop away and become less important.

You don't have to make amends if you were the one at fault—but you may find yourself drawn to do just that.

Above all, when you are working in this layer or level of the Divine, do not be surprised if miracles occur, such as in these examples:

- A woman loves her alcoholic boyfriend but wants him to get sober. Even after nagging and threatening for years, nothing works. She speaks to him using telepathy, soul to soul, and tells him how she feels. She also hears his answers telepathically—why he's in so much emotional pain, and why he self-medicates with alcohol. Within a week, he's decided to enroll in a treatment program.
- A man fears that his wife's frequent work travel is causing marital problems. She loves him, but she also loves her job. He speaks to her soul to soul, and a few days later she receives an offer for a better job that doesn't require as much travel.
- A woman suspects her husband of infidelity. She gets up the nerve to speak to him soul to soul, and discovers that he hasn't been cheating at all, but he has been as miserable in the relationship as she has. They separate amicably a year later, relieved to go their separate ways.
- A man discovers he has cancer and wants to make amends with his brother, from whom he's been estranged for thirty years. He speaks soul to soul to him, and within a week his brother has flown out to take care of him during his treatment.

These stories are a small handful of what happens when I teach clients how to speak soul to soul to the ones they love (or currently hate!) the most. It doesn't replace in-person communication. But when communication has gone awry, or the parties involved are too hurt or too stubborn, it can be the one solution that brings healing, love, and peace back into the relationship.

Healing with energetic cords

You can also heal relationships using *energetic cords*.

You've probably heard of cords before; it's common for people working in healing to talk about energetic connections between people as cords. This is especially true when the connection is a negative one, as in "I really need to cut those cords with my ex."

It's an interesting idea—that we're all linked together like mountaineers with energetic belay ropes. But are there really cords of energy between people?

Once again, we're at the point where "cords" or "ropes" or "strings" can't be seen under a microscope, with a telescope, with an x-ray, or with super-high-power-night-vision goggles! Does this mean that they don't exist? Well, as you already know from the exercises you've done in the last few chapters, scientific proof will just have to wait. We're pioneers—we work with what works. And using energetic cords to heal relationship works like a dream.

My own explanation of energetic cords is based on what I have seen when working with clients—basically, that cords are energetic connections between people, objects, or spaces. I call them cords because:

- That's what my spirit guides call them.
- That's what they're called in the channeled writing I receive.
- They visually look like cords—they appear as energetic strands or rope or yarn.
- They act like cords—they can be cut, attached, looped, unraveled.

Cords? Strands? Sort of sounds like the verbiage we use when we talk about string theory, no? Hmmmm. Well, being 100 percent practical psychic pioneer and 0 percent quantum physicist, all I can say is I'm not quite sure how cords work—but I know that they do work.

How cords present

Like most everything else intuitive, you see cords in your mind's eye. This is nice, because if you saw cords with your eyes open, everyone would be covered in a tangle of rope! Cords can be health or unhealthy, embedded or on the surface, connecting or cut loose. Some examples might be:

- A client who is experiencing problems with unresolved pain presents as having cords tangled throughout her body. When I begin to remove them energetically (by raising vibration and then allowing guides and angels to do this work through me), her energetic body flails and screams as they are removed. I remove perhaps two hundred of these cords! Some of them snap off midway, like a worm might break as you pull it out of the earth. These cords, which I suspect are yucky entity energies, appear like white worms or spaghetti. After the session, the client reports feeling "nothing," but notes that she's exhausted. She goes home and sleeps for twelve hours straight. When she wakes up, she emails to tell me that her pain has decreased by 80 percent, and she feels as if something has "released."

- A client who has split from her boyfriend comes to me, and I see that energetically she is enslaved by the cords of her ex. During the session, she reports that her hands and feet are bound with thick ropes, such as the cabled rope used to tie off boats. I call in angels and guides, and they begin to saw the ropes off. It takes a long time; the cords to her ex are astonishingly thick and heavy. Once the cords are off her ankles and wrists, she notices that there are cords extending through her heart, and wrapping all over her torso. These are slowly removed by the Divine. At the conclusion of the session, she feels the presence of a multitude of angels standing near, pouring healing light onto her body until she is immersed in healing and wholeness. Later, she writes to tell me that her problems with her ex have dissolved; she is no longer afraid of him.

- Two close friends come for a reading, together. They are dressed almost identically, and when I ask them about this, they laugh and say, "This always happens to us." They're even wearing identical necklaces. As I look into their energy, I see that their heart cords are fully attached to each other, and present as glowing pillars of light. I understand from this how deeply they are connected, both in this present life and in all past and future lives. I encourage them to work together, and to start a business in addition to their friendship—they are energetically attached in a very healthy way, and will do well spending time together.

- A mother longs to connect with her estranged daughter. In session work, I first have her connect to her daughter soul to soul, and tell her that she would like to heal the relationship. Then, I have the woman create a heart cord, a channel of white dazzling light, which she attaches to her daughter's heart. Within seconds, the mother is sobbing, saying she's never felt her daughter as closely as that. She runs home to call her on the phone, and the two resolve their issues through tears and laughter.

- A man has a problem with his boss. I look into the situation energetically, and see that his boss is continually cutting any cords that the man tries to attach to him. I ask the man about this, and he admits that yes, he has been trying to "suck up" to his boss, in hopes of getting a promotion. We do an exercise in which the man removes all lingering cords from his boss with the help of his spirit guides. The energy between them now glows in a healthy, clean way. Three months later, the man writes to say that his boss has created a new position just for him—and it's much better than the original job he was hoping for.

- A woman wants to lose weight. Working together, we do a session in which she cuts cords from her past, overweight self, and attaches them to herself in the future—a thin self. She is stunned to notice that after repeating this process daily for a week, she's no longer eating compulsively.

As you can see from these examples, cords present in different ways:

- As wormlike, tangled, invasive, unhealthy cords that take a while to be cleared, pulled out, or removed

- As thick, binding, unhealthy cords that need to be cut

- As a lovely channel or column of beautiful light from one to another, often from heart to heart or forehead to forehead

- As simple cords that we attach to another (or that another attaches to us); these may be healthy, unhealthy, or neutral

- As simple cords that we attach to ourselves: past and future versions

As always, you can remove or attach cords simply, easily, and elegantly simply by holding this intention in your mind. If you're having trouble, step aside and let your guides and angels do the work for you.

Healing with vibrational alignment

Vibrational alignment sounds fancy. Another way to think of it is as energetic or vibrational matching. The idea is to "tune" or "align" yourself so that your energetic vibration is the same as that of the person you'd like to heal your relationship with.

This method is especially useful for quick fixes, such as squabbling, bickering, getting angry with someone for no reason, that kind of thing. Basically, by matching energy with another person, you allow the energy between you to rebalance or reset—almost like a kind of energetic release valve.

I like to work with the concepts of color (as we did in chapter 5), when I'm doing vibrational alignment. For example, let's say I'm dealing with someone who's irate. Maybe they're mad at me; maybe they're mad at the world. Who knows? They're just mad—and I can feel it!

I look quickly into our vibrational alignment, and if I'm using color as my tool, I scan or notice what color the other person's body is presenting energetically. Let's say it's red, but my body is presenting blue. I'll quickly shift my body to red, to be in vibrational alignment with this other person. Instantly, I will notice that we are in better accord—we understand each other better.

A quick note: vibrational alignment doesn't mean that if someone else is in a deep, dark, emo kind of mood that you need to go there! "Mood" or "emotion" has nothing to do with vibrational alignment. Mood is emotional, which dips and sways all over the place, all the time. Energy is simply what we are. When you match yourself to the energetic vibration of another, you simply become more aware of your Oneness.

And that, of course, changes everything.

Exercise: Healing Relationships

Healing relationships with other people is easy, when you use energy. You can use each of these techniques—(a) soul-to-soul communication, (b) energetic cords, or (c) vibrational alignment—on its own, or you can mix them up and use a little of everything all at once. As always, your guides are there to help and support you at every step; you never have to go it alone.

1. Do your setup, as described on page 13.

2. Go up to level three, until you are in the place where you can easily communicate with your spirit guides and angels.

3. Call in the person you wish to heal your relationship with.

4. Speak to them soul to soul, and see what happens. Allow your guides and angels to assist as much as they'd like. As you communicate soul to soul, remember that you may receive information-embedded emotional messages that heal. Once you're done communicating with this person (you'll know when you're done), simply thank them and return to earth reality. Watch for signs and shifts in the relationship in the next days and weeks. You will be surprised how quickly this technique works!

5. If you are working with energetic cords, ask your guides to show you the cords between you and this person. Notice how they present. Then, with your guides' assistance, remove, cut, or attach cords as needed. Often, the guides will do all of this work for you; you will simply witness what they are doing. When you are certain that your energy is clear, thank your guides and the other person, and come back to earth reality. In most cases, you will feel an immediate difference in your body, as if something has been released or healed. Watch for signs and shifts in the relationship in the coming days and weeks.

6. If you are working with vibrational alignment, you probably won't be in a situation where you can do your setup. You may be working on the fly! Simply notice the color of the person you're having trouble with, and match your own energy to this vibration. Simply

think "match" or ask your guides to do it for you. It's very fast, and very easy. Pay attention to how differently you feel when you are in vibrational alignment with another person.

7. As an experiment, take a day and practice vibrational alignment with every person you meet that day. You may be stunned at how friendly, harmonious, and nice people are to you that day!

Remember you are One, and remember also this: whatever affects the smallest, whatever affects the least, also affects you. You are not merely interconnected; you are the same.

—The Messages

---

fourteen

Healing Relationships Beyond Time

Healing that takes place in any realm affects all realms.
This is the law of One. With every aspect that is healed,
all aspects are healed.

—The Messages

It's tough enough dealing with relationships with those who are living—all those spouses, partners, parents, kids, friends, colleagues, acquaintances, and enemies roaming around on this planet at the same time you are!

But what happens when the relationship that's causing you problems isn't with a living person? What happens when the relationship is with someone who's departed—a person you know who's transitioned into another realm? And, maybe you don't even know this person—maybe they're some long-lost ancestor, a great-great-great grandmother or grandfather who never did anything for you except provide you with the genetics for that distinctive nose, hairline, or body shape.

The reason these relationships with the departed affect us so much is that relationships are *karmic*. That's right—karmic!

Now, not everyone believes in karma, and even more people don't agree on exactly what karma is. It's an ancient concept that's been adapted by many creeds and belief systems. That said, for the purpose of clearest communication, I'm going to use the word *karma* in a particular way, as advised to me by my guides: *Karma is soul lessons learned over time.* This includes soul lessons learned by one person, learned via a relationship between people, or learned by whole groups of people over time.

You see, even though we get to choose who our parents are before we come into this world as beautiful bawling souls, in that same act of soul choice, we also choose the people from whom we've come. Our lineage. Our ancestors. Our family tree. And this choice is a karmic choice.

Sometimes, the question begs—what were our souls thinking?

For example, on my father's side of the family I'm descended from Norwegian royalty—I've been to their tiny village in Norway and seen the family name recorded in a tattered, leather-bound book, extending as far back as the Vikings. It sounds kind of cool, doesn't it? I mean, Norwegian royalty! But, study a little history and you'll soon discover that Vikings were teeming with bad behavior, such as:

- Sailing off to "discover" new lands and claiming them as their own, even though said new lands were already fully populated by native peoples
- Heading out for raping and pillaging
- Other unmentionable acts of barbarity that really were not very nice indeed

Okay, so it was the Middle Ages. But these actions created a whole lot of karma for this side of the family.

I know what you're thinking—well, at least she can always rely on her maternal side! But on my mom's side, it was absolutely no better. Poverty combined with extreme fertility—I'm talking thirteen kids, dirt floors, no central heat, one-potato-in-the-pantry-to-feed-everyone-for-a-whole-day kind of poverty—seemed to be the theme for generation after generation. The photos reveal the situation pretty clearly: there are my ancestors, tight-lipped, grim-faced, hardscrabble people who came from Germany and Ireland, then settled unhappily in the Midwest. Early marriage, miscarriages, still births, scarlet fever, corporal punishment, and the fervent belief that God was punishing them for their sins—this kind of thought pattern prevailing as recently as two generations back, during the Great Depression.

Sigh.

There's a tad bit of karma here, too.

What happens when ancestor lines are loaded with unresolved karma (and pretty much every family's is) is that you—the great-grand-daughter or great-grandson or whatever relative you are—are affected by what this group of ancestors put into motion during their lifetime. Their actions, their mistakes, their successes. All of it.

In former times, this concept had heady, punitive names, such as "sins of the fathers" or "marked by the gypsy's curse." However, what they didn't know then (and what we do know now) is that the "sin" or "curse"—two concepts I don't believe in, by the way—can be fixed or resolved or completed, now, in present time, by anyone in the ancestral line.

That person could even be you.

Karma—and again, by this I mean soul lessons learned over time, and not punishments, curses, bad luck, or whatever negative attri-butes some people attach to it—continues from one generation to the next until someone, somewhere along the line, finally fixes it. Some-one finally recognizes the soul lesson, or can look with detachment and compassion at the past, and see what their ancestors were going through as they tried to learn this soul lesson. And with this attention, they are able to fix the karmic issue. With this understanding, they are able to heal this karmic issue for themselves—as well as for those who came before, and all future generations to come.

It sounds a little confusing, but remember, time is not linear. The way we perceive it is in seconds, minutes, days, weeks, years. But in truth, we actually exist in all time. The past, the present, the future—

they exist simultaneously, all happening in the Now. Thus when you heal the past, you also heal the present, and the future.

Present. Past. Future.

All healed instantaneously.

In one fell swoop.

This method of healing, what I might broadly call *transdimensional healing*, has been explored in many cultures. Shamanism works in this area. Native American traditions explore this with the idea of seven generations. In Western culture, Bert Hellinger was a pioneer in working in this field; his methodology was called *family constellations therapy*. Because many of Hellinger's clients were of northern European descent, his work uncovered a great deal of the karma many experienced in their ancestry surrounding World War II, especially the tremendous negative energy brought forward by the Nazis. I would expect that anyone whose ancestors lived in a country terrorized by war would find similar karmic trauma.

Remember that we are all connected. Not just in the here and now, but across all boundaries of time and space. We are one with our ancestors, generations back. We are also one with our ancestors to come, generations ahead. What we do in this lifetime affects relationships backward and forward, as well as in present time.

Gives you chills, doesn't it?

It is the simplest thing, to jump levels between dimensions of past, present, future. In healing across time, there is no time that is too late.

—The Messages

Karmic healing

Karmic healing in this way uses the skills of mediumship that you learned in chapter 12. It works by healing the relationship between the living and the departed. In a recent session, two sisters came to me. Born and raised in Spain, they'd been best friends as kids. Now, as adults, both had the oppressive feeling that something was "not quite right" from their past—a pervasive, ugly feeling of abuse or molestation. They asked me to look into the past, in hopes that whatever had happened to them might be revealed. As often happens, I began to receive information about these clients before they arrived for their appointment. The sisters, my guides told me, hadn't been abused physically or sexually. However, there was emotional abuse rampant in the family. The question now, was why.

To facilitate the process, I had the sisters each separately draw a simple diagram of their family on a piece of paper—this included their current spouse and children, their family of origin, grandparents, and anyone else who came to mind, living or departed. As the sisters diagrammed their ancestry, they mentioned one particular family member, and suddenly the energy in the room got very, very thick. Heavy, intense, unpleasant; it settled around us unhappily, and I knew a departed spirit would make himself or herself known soon.

I took the sisters into trance, called in my own guide to act as a bouncer, and sure enough, within seconds, a spirit presented. He was an older man, dressed in a black or charcoal suit, with the strong smell of cigarettes around him. Not just smoke either, but the dark, sooty smell of old ashtrays—the worst kind of dark, ugly, low vibration. This was the family member in question—the sisters' father.

As soon as the entity presented, I experienced his pain full force—it coursed through my body in a shockingly strong way, to the point of physically throwing me backward in my chair. Here was the family member who had been severely abused during his own childhood. Terror and shame washed over me, as I felt his emotional messaging.

During this time, the sisters also experienced this presence, though in a less intense way—the emotion all coursed through me, and I felt it as if I were this man. Within minutes, it all became clear: this relative's experience of abuse as a child had affected him into adulthood—and his deep emotional wound had affected the lives of his own children. Looking further into the past, I also saw that this man had been one in a long line of abused. This particular karma extended back for generations into the family.

I asked the sisters if they were able to have compassion for this man. They agreed, and telepathically stated their feelings to this entity. Instantaneously, the cigarette smell dissipated, and the oppressive feelings of terror and pain receded. Soon, the room was swirling with an intensive healing energy felt by both the sisters and the entity. The family energy had been cleared. Not just for the past, but also for the future.

As is certainly clear from this story, this kind of work is intensive— it's not for the faint of heart. I do not suggest that you attempt this level of work on your own, unless you've found someone to train or mentor you. But this kind of work is possible, and the healing it offers is profound.

Unresolved issues

Abuse, addiction, accidents—such is the stuff that family karma seems to revolve around. And it just makes sense. When we think of karma as soul lessons learned over time, it's obvious that before a human can rise into consciousness, he or she must confront the deepest, darkest core. Most of us tackle the small stuff easily enough during our lifetimes—we learn as we go. But when the really big stuff comes up, as it inevitably does, having the courage to face it can be a truly heroic act.

Another example of karmic healing across time involved Jacqueline, a middle-aged professional woman. For decades, Jacqueline had been captivated by a departed aunt on her mother's side. She'd never met the woman but had seen a photo of her in her twenties. She was compelled to know more.

By the time Jacqueline came to me, she'd quite fully researched this departed soul: she knew her name, her history, and had even visited her grave. "She's trying to tell me something," Jacqueline told me, and I agreed.

In session, I took Jacqueline into trance, called up my guides, and very soon the departed woman came forth in period clothing, bringing with her a strong scent of flowers. Her urgency, she told us, was not about her, but that of a child—and as she mentioned the child, she immediately appeared beside her. It was a girl of about two. Next, I saw clairvoyantly a "movie" of the girl walking alone by a river—and I watched as she slipped and fell into the river. In session, Jacqueline and I both fully experienced the intensive, embedded emotional meaning of the situation: shock, pain, overwhelming grief by the family.

"No one in my family knew my aunt had a daughter; this little girl had been forgotten," she said, adding, "My aunt came back to tell her story." By allowing Divine illumination of the situation, Jacqueline was able to illuminate and heal the past that had been hidden for so long.

In a third case, Lisa, a woman in her forties, was suffering from intense sadness; even as our session began, she burst into tears as she told me of her plight. Her family was gone: she'd lost her grandfather, mother, and brother in the space of one year. The grief was insurmountable. "I have no one left on this earth," she said. Even though all had died of natural causes, the loss was so unexpected that she was still in shock. More than anything, she longed to communicate with them once again.

As I took Lisa into trance and we stepped up in vibration, my guide came forth with one of her departed relatives. However, to the client's surprise, this was not her grandfather, mother, or brother—but her grandmother, who had transitioned twelve years earlier.

"They're here with me," the grandmother said. "They didn't mean to leave you; it was just their time. But," she added slowly and clearly, to ensure her message was heard, "it's not your time yet."

As the client cried out her loneliness, in great heaving sobs, the grandmother simply came and stood in front of her, and offered her an object—a book. I directed the client to open the book, and as she paged through the book, she saw and experienced scenes of tremendous joy in her life—all the fun and family times with the relatives who had departed. She cried out more, in love and pain.

But then . . . there was more. The pages continued into the future, and scenes she didn't understand started to appear: there was herself with a family, including a man and younger children. They weren't her kids—or were they? Scenes she didn't understand continued to present, of herself surrounded by young children. As she looked through the book, her heart became lighter and lighter. "There's a beautiful life ahead for you," her grandmother said calmly. "Be patient."

In this case, the client did not karmically heal the past. Instead, it was the grandmother, a departed spirit from the past, who came forward to help heal the future, sending comfort in the dark hours of grief, promising that the light was yet to come.

Healing family relationships

For most of us, family relationships aren't perfect. Sometimes, there's a misunderstanding, or an argument that takes place, and we never resolve that issue before the person dies. The things we wanted to say don't get said. The problem is, unless this energy is released, cleared, and attended to, this sort of unresolved stuff tends to go dark and deep pretty fast.

Illumination is the only cure—by shining the Divine light upon the problem or issue.

We all know that it's important to say what you need to say to people before they pass. It's important for them, and it's also important for you. Yet often we're stubborn. Or they're stubborn. Or there's so much water under the proverbial relationship bridge, it all seems too little, too late.

Of course, it's not.

As it happens, soul growth often results when we resolve issues with those who are departing and those who have departed. This includes:

- Clearing up misunderstandings
- Holding compassion for another person's experience
- Asking for forgiveness for any harm you've done
- Forgiving others for any harm they've done
- Saying thank you for the times you've shared
- Saying "I love you"

But, sometimes, we just . . . can't. Even if we want to, or know that it will solve everything, we just . . . don't. Sometimes our reasons are geographical—we've lived apart for so long, we've forgotten that we are in relationship to this person who is our mother, father, brother, sister.

We haven't lived in the same house with them for decades; we speak to them on the phone less and less often. The relationship is distant—not vibrant, active, alive. We have forgotten how we know each other.

Sometimes, our reasons are due to time running out: we get that dreaded call in the middle of the night, and the person we mean to clear thing ups with, well—they're gone. They've passed over, without us ever having time to say what we really wanted to say.

Other times, there's so much hurt and pain surrounding our relationship with this person that we carry around emotions that fester until they're a giant monster of pain. It hurts to bring this monster out of the closet. So we don't.

And sometimes, we simply miss the person who has passed on; we've cleared up our stuff with them, and yet there is still love: we love them, they love us, we understand we both did the best we could. Yet there's still more to say. Even after they're gone, we want to say, and feel, and experience more with this person.

Fortunately, all of these situations surrounding relationship with the departed can be healed, even if we are not in the same physical realm.

Laura's father died when she was an adult, leaving behind a successful company. Laura was chosen to manage the company after his death, based on her years of working with him there. A few years later, her mother was diagnosed with cancer, and was told she would live only a few more months. During this time, the economy shifted and the company struggled for the first time. Laura felt strongly it would rebound. However, her mother was incensed by the change: "Your father built that company with his bare hands; now you're running it to the ground," she blurted in a rage just before her death. Laura was too stunned to reply. A few days later, her mother passed.

During our session, I called forth my guide, and immediately a departed spirit also came forward. It wasn't Laura's mother, as she'd hoped. Instead, it was her father, who appeared in an enormous amount of suffering—he relayed that he had tried very hard to convince Laura's mother that she was acting incorrectly, but she refused to listen. "Her mind," he said, holding his own head in his hands and showing Laura the pain. "She was so sick; she didn't know what she was saying." Laura listened, tears streaming down her face.

Then, he held out something to Laura—a shiny silver trophy, the same kind you'd give a child. "You're a winner," her dad said, beaming at her.

I asked Laura to ask her guides to connect her heart to her father's heart, and she was able to fully feel the love her dad has for her. With an audible gasp, she slammed back in her chair as this emotional energy flooded into her. When that experience was complete, she was so emotionally filled that she was unable to speak; we came out of trance and I ended the session.

The shift in Laura was beyond description. The smile on her face almost lifted her out of the chair, and she appeared to be surrounded with a glowing yellow aura. I asked her if she still needed to say anything to her mother, and she answered simply and clearly, "My mother didn't have her faculties at the end. She didn't mean what she said. I understand that now."

She went out that afternoon and bought herself a shiny silver trophy, and put it on her desk at work. Within months, the company experienced a surge of growth and was back on its feet. Now, whenever she feels hesitant about a business decision, she simply calls upon her father to encourage and advise her. The love he continues to have for her, and the love that he translated for her mother, have changed Laura's life.

Karmic healing is instantaneous

Time after time, I have seen results similar to Laura's. When there is finally deep understanding—not just intellectual understanding, but an understanding accompanied by the embedded emotional meaning communicated by the departed that includes love, bliss, caring, nurturing, and forgiveness—healing is instantaneous. There is a complete shift in the client, as they experience full emotional connection.

Even if communication with the departed leads to the experience of the departed's own negative emotions—pain, confusion, illness, worry, and so forth—it still allows the client to hold a deep compassion around the departed's experiences. This understanding facilitates healing across all layers and levels of time: present, past, future.

In either case, this healing is instantaneous.

Why instantaneous? Because this is how energy works. When we are working in the highest vibrations of love and light, when we are deeply connected to the etheric realm where our guides and angels are, we are infused with a kind of energy that lifts us up, and moves up beyond the confines of linear time. There is no waiting period with the Divine, or with Divine healing. Instead, it arrives as pure energy of love and light, and it transforms us instantly as we receive it.

Exercise: Healing Beyond Time

Healing your relationship with the departed can be intensively emotional. You may want to work with another person for support, or you may prefer to work on your own. Either way, do be prepared for the intensity of emotion you will feel.

1. Do your setup, as described on page 13.

2. Rise to level three and meet your guides. Then, ask your guides who will be assisting you today, and notice as this guide steps forward in front of you.

3. Ask your guide to help you connect and heal with the departed you want to heal with, and then wait to see who comes forward— this may be the departed you're thinking of. Or it may be someone else who steps forward on this person's behalf.

4. Ask questions of the departed, or ask your guide to do so. Allow yourself to receive answers, in all ways they present.

5. Once the main messaging has been received, ask your guide to create a heart connection between you and the departed if this feels right. Or, ask your guide to provide a method of healing. The ways in which this happens are varied, interesting, and lovely. Accept this gift of healing.

6. Regardless of what has happened—positive, negative, clearing, or confusing—understand that you are healed, and that your relationship with the departed has been transformed.

7. As you come out of trance and return to earth reality, notice how you feel: relieved, overwhelmed, stunned, comforted, cared for, shocked, loved.

8. Spend some time journaling about this experience.

9. Notice how you think differently about the departed in the weeks and months to come. Notice also how other relationships surrounding the departed have been transformed or are transforming.

In this lifetime, healing may be yours to grant to those who have come before, to those who will come after. Watch for this; seek to understand if this is your task.

—The Messages

---

fifteen

Attracting Love

In the meeting of true lover, true Beloved, the energy becomes
more saturated, more full. In this space,
there is the creation of a third force, which is Divine.
—The Messages

"How's your relationship?" we might ask a friend over coffee, hoping to hear some juicy news. Our question isn't just about any relationship, of course—it's about a romantic relationship. Leaning forward over our triple-mocha-no-whip, we're dying to hear the dish on who's dating whom, who's sleeping with whom, and if such activities are progressing to the categories of *partner* or *spouse*.

We use the term *relationship* this way all the time. But in truth, we're always in relationship to each other all the time, even if not one iota of romance is involved. Even as you read this, you are in relationship to someone: the person sitting next to you at the bus, the person across the room at a café, the waitress who serves your table . . . and so on.

We know this—sort of. Yet we're still hung up on the idea of finding that one special, star-crossed guy or gal whose name is d-e-s-t-i-n-y.

We're obsessed with it, this idea of "true love" or soul mate. We buy our clothes and even our cars in hopes of attracting it; we slap on certain colognes or underarm deodorants in hopes of creating the ideal waft of pheromones to attract this special someone.

We're crazy for romantic relationships because, frankly, it's in our DNA. As humans, we instinctively look for mates—that's how the human race stays alive, through procreation of the species. We're also crazy for romantic relationships because so much of our environment—including our culture, background, education, media, social networking, and peer pressure—is geared to this idea of finding "the one."

But there's another reason we crave love, in addition to instinct and environment. Energetically, we're obsessed with love relationships, because romantic relationships are always karmic. Of course, every relationship on Earth and every relationship beyond time and space is karmic—but the karma of romantic relationships is stronger, more significant, and more noticeable to the parties involved.

How do you know it's love?

I'd like to say it's all about hearts and flowers, champagne and chocolate—but, in most cases, the idea of romantic love for adults is defined by one thing: physical intimacy. After all, humans aren't plants—the last time I checked, we can't reproduce asexually! We're humans, and that means (with the exception of modern reproductive technologies) we don't reproduce alone.

I'm certainly not saying you have to reproduce to be in love!

But the must-create-an-heir factor is steeped pretty deep into our psyches—after all, it's how we arrive into this world. First, there's the whole sperm-meets-egg routine, performed by our mother and father months before we knew 'em. Next, we progressed as cellular energy, dividing and conquering until we were big enough to live inside our mother's body for nine-plus months. Finally, we entered earth reality in perhaps the most physically intimate way possible—straight from the womb. The kicker? Many of us were breast-fed by this exact same body we were pushed out of, for months and sometimes years.

This is intimate, physically connected life in the most human way possible. It's skin on skin, breath on breath, two bodies creating and then one body housing and feeding another human being.

Miraculous, yes?

Psychologists have said we always seek the mother or the father in our love relationships, and from what I've seen, I won't argue. These early relationships and how they play out are crucial to our development. But by the time you're an adult, at whatever age that happens for you, you understand that you are no longer controlled by your parents, and that the first relationship that contained just you and your mother and/or father isn't going to be the relationship that sustains you any longer. At some point, you'll be ready to step outside your initial family circle to develop your own relationships, and create your own life.

And that's where the fun starts.

Karmic crossings

The idea of destined romantic love has been around since before medieval times, and the concept has reinvented itself over the centuries. Today, the term is most likely to contain the ideas of:

- Your one and only
- Your true love
- Your soul mate
- Your destiny
- Love at first sight

These are all nice, romanticized terms for what is energetically referred to as a primary soul mate who is also a romantic partner. These significant soul matings exist to teach you the lessons of your heart, either easily and gently—or painfully and carelessly.

No matter what your age, you can look back and determine the love relationships that were the big *karmic crossing*. In positive relationships, you might have been working on issues such as:

- Trust
- Love
- Affection
- Openness
- Building together
- Patience
- Compatibility
- Selflessness

In negative or lesser relationships, you might have been working on:

- Power
- Control
- Betrayal
- Addiction
- Abuse
- Anger
- Abandonment

In either case, these karmic crossings helped you to move forward on your path of soul growth.

Do we just have one soul mate?

Officially, just as we have multiple and myriad relationships with all kinds of people, we also have multiple and myriad soul mates. Everyone's a soul mate, at some level or another.

But I know what you mean. You're talking about the one special person for you in your life—the one you're destined to meet, and the one who's going to change your life, be the butter on your bread, the honey in your tea, and so forth.

Your primary soul mate.

Most of us have at least one of these soul mates in our lifetime.

Often, we have a few.

In this day and age, we're all accustomed to people having serial relationships over time. Very few people marry at eighteen and stay together until death at eighty-eight anymore. With divorce rates hovering at 50 percent and fewer people getting married at all, the idea of one lifetime relationship is just not part of our culture anymore. Nowadays, it's likely that people will have several partners in a lifetime. So, what happens when we meet someone who we think is a soul mate—but, over time, the relationship doesn't work out? You split up, and then eventually, you meet another person who you are certain is your soul mate.

Does this mean your first partner or spouse wasn't a soul mate?

No, it doesn't. Both your past and current partner were soul mates. It's just that the first soul mate you were with helped you learn a particular set of lessons. Once those lessons were learned, it was time to jump levels to a more advanced set of lessons, with the new soul mate.

Our soul mates always match us where we are, in terms of our consciousness and heart expansion. You know the saying "Like attracts like"? Well, that's how it works. When you're immature and not very conscious, you attract a soul mate who's at the same place in his/her development. When you jump levels and expand into more awareness, you meet a soul mate who can meet and match you there.

That also means that once your karmic crossing is complete—once you've learned the soul lessons you've been put together to learn—then the relationship is also complete.

You're ready to move forward and learn new lessons, with another partner.

Does this mean the first soul mate wasn't "real"? Not at all. Most adults have been in profoundly significant relationships that "didn't work out" over time. It's not because you didn't love the person at the time, or because the person wasn't your soul mate. It's just that for most of us in modern culture, there's going to be more than one karmic crossing in a lifetime.

Now, of course there are still people who meet in high school and stay in love until death in old age. If you are one of these people, consider yourself fantastically gifted by the Universe! You have a chance to learn soul lessons over decades with one single person by your side. This is wonderful.

But if you're like most of us who've been married and divorced, partnered and de-partnered, please allow yourself to understand that there is always plenty of time to attract a new soul mate to you, should you wish this.

And when you do meet this person—whether you are in your thirties, your fifties, or your eighties—remember that meeting a soul mate is a gift. Accept the gift, and say "thank you." Don't dither and dally and second-guess. Unwrap the package!

When you meet your Beloved for the first time, your energy finds its vibrational match. This is why you feel recognition, a sense of knowing. In this way, when you meet your match, you have found your mate.

—The Messages

Meeting a soul mate is gift

When you meet a soul mate, you know it. There's an immediate sense of recognition, not of the person's physical self, which is different in this lifetime than it was in the past lifetimes you were together, but in their core personality. You just know them, and in many cases you know them very, very well.

Charla was in her forties when she met Marcus, a sculptor whose work was being shown in a top gallery. Walking past one day, she saw one of his sculptures through the window, and to her surprise, she felt a shock of immediate recognition. "I'd seen it before," she told me in our session. "I can't explain how, but it was very familiar."

In fact, she was so intrigued by the sculpture that when Marcus held a gallery showing the next month, she made sure she attended. To her surprise, he was much older than she was—twenty-four years older, to be exact. Still, she summoned her nerve and introduced herself. To say that they hit it off that evening was an understatement. "I felt as if we were covered in a kind of sparkly cloud the whole night," she told me.

On their second date he proposed, and Charla accepted without hesitation. "I hadn't known him long—but I knew him inside out," she said. "I'd been looking for him my whole life, and I wasn't about to miss this chance." Charla understood the importance of accepting the gift of a soul mate, when it presents. If she'd been put off by their age difference, this opportunity might have passed.

When the Universe is swirling in your favor, all systems are go, and everything says "yes," it's a good time for you to say "yes," too.

What meeting a soul mate feels like

When you meet a soul mate, you'll feel instantly at ease and comfortable with them, as if you've known them for a very long time. Which, of course, you have. However, they may not be at all what you thought you wanted!

Time and again, clients tell me of meeting primary soul mates who present much different from those they expected: they're older, younger, a different race, a different culture, a different hairstyle. They're the perfect love match, but they don't look anything like what you ordered! Moreover, there's always a compellingly strong attraction, even if you wouldn't normally have been attracted to that type of person—there's an amazing need to be together, and an almost physical pain if you must be apart.

And then, there is the energy. This can take the form of visible energy, such as white flashes, lightning bolts, auras, and so forth, as the Universe attempts to draw your attention to the convergence of primary soul mates that is happening.

For example, my client Anna did some energy work with me to call forth her soul mate. Soon after, she met a new co-worker at a staff meeting, and the minute they shook hands, she felt dizzy. "My knees went weak; I actually had to excuse myself and sit down," she explained. Ron wasn't particularly her type, so she brushed her reaction aside: he was nine years younger, and he was blond, even though she preferred dark-haired men. "I thought I had the flu, actually," she laughed.

But then she started to bump into Ron multiple times a day, almost as if she were a Ron magnet. "It didn't make sense why I was seeing him so often, and in such odd places," she said. A few weeks later, she was in the employee kitchen heating up her lunch, and who should walk in but Ron. As they chatted in the room together, "a bolt of lightning leaped across from his body to mine," she said. "It was bright white, about ten inches tall, and extended the full eight feet between us. I gasped, and when I looked at him, his mouth was hanging open and he looked stunned."

The next day, Ron came up to her office and asked her if she'd like to have coffee. She said yes, and four months later they were living together.

Energy in love relationships

Energy presents the same way in soul-mate relationships as it does in any relationship—it's just stronger, more intense, and easier to recognize. Some of the common ways energy presents when you are meeting your soul mate are:

- Vibrational matching
- Energetic cording
- Aura blending
- Symbiotic healing

Vibrational matching

When people first discover they are soul mates, the first sensation is often that of recognition—the idea that they've met before. Of course, they have met before, in all the past lives they've had together. But this sense of recognition also comes from the fact that they are experiencing a vibrational match in their energy.

One way to think about it might be as a color or word, as we've done before. For example, some people vibrate as "orange, relaxed," say, while others vibrate at "green, happy." No problem with either color or word; neither is better or worse than another. But if you are an "orange, relaxed," then you are going to feel most comfortable with someone else who is also vibrating "orange, relaxed."

Vibrational matching also relates to consciousness, which hopefully increases and expands as a person lives and grows. This is why you might feel that you have "outgrown" someone or "moved beyond" them, common terms used by people who've partnered and then split.

"I kept asking myself if this is all there was," said Jamie, a client in her late thirties who was in the process of divorcing her husband of thirteen years. "I seemed to be growing by leaps and bounds, and he wasn't. He didn't seem to have any awareness of who I was."

If you are feeling out of synch with your love relationship, check your vibrational match. Is the person vibrating at a lower level than you? Are you vibrating at a lower level than your partner? In order to check, simply open your awareness and enter in. If you're vastly different, take a moment and attempt to vibrationally match your partner. If he's "orange," see if you can match "orange." As you explore this process, notice if your attempt to vibrationally match your partner leaves you feeling uncomfortable, unhappy, or physically drained. If so, it's probably a signal that your vibrational match has shifted—and it's a good idea to take a closer look and explore why.

Energetic cording

Cording refers to the energetic ties we place on and/or accept from other people. Cording isn't good or bad, but sometimes it can get out of balance. Often in relationships where power, control, and abandonment are big issues, cording can get pretty intense. It's as if one person is lassoing another person with hundreds of energetic cords—not very comfortable if you're the person being looped! And not particularly healthy for the person doing the looping, either.

Jack met Anita when she was twenty-two; he was thirty-one. He was afraid that at her young age she wouldn't be able to stay true to him, and so he looped her with possessive energy—he wrapped her up in energetic cords so thick she couldn't breathe, hoping that these would secure their relationship. Of course, it didn't work that way. In order to have a love relationship at a high vibrational match, you can't suffocate a person in energetic cording! Anita moved out after four years of living together, saying she needed some time and space to think things through. Jack panicked, and requested a session with me to "find out how he could get her back." The energetic imbalance between them presented instantly, and I told him that his extensive cording had, in effect, caused the relationship to suffer.

In session, I helped Jack enter in and then began to energetically remove the cords that he had attached to Anita—there were literally hundreds of them. As he worked, he also noticed that she had wrapped some cords around him, too, but in a looser way. After much discussion, he agreed to remove these as well. By the end of the session, he felt noticeably lighter and brighter. "I don't need to control her so she'll love me," he said. "I don't want a person that loves only because they're forced to."

The result of this cord-releasing for Anita was fast: she met and married a new man and became pregnant within a few months. This was stunning to Jack, but it also helped him see how truly their relationship was over. He took his time before entering a new relationship—he didn't date for a year, and when he did meet a new woman, he made sure that the energetic cording, both from him and to him, was at a more balanced level.

Aura blending

Usually, *aura* refers to the energetic field of a person—it's the energy that surrounds and pervades our physical body. We can expand or contract our auras at any time, simply by holding awareness of the energy and requesting that this happen. Usually, our auras stick to us like Peter Pan's shadow; but sometimes, when we are very close to another person, such as a soul mate, our auras will blend. This is closely tied to Eastern ideas of Tantra, Kundalini, and other energetic concepts of love. When a couple is deeply connected on a karmic level, and deeply in vibrational match, they may present with one aura—two people who have merged as one. This kind of couple will often be fully corded together as well.

You may have seen this kind of blending in couples who've been together a long time, or in those who are extremely in love and physically intertwined (often right in front of you!). But you'll also see this in everyday couples who have just participated in very intensely connective and emotional activities, such as having sex.

Aura blending isn't always related to sex, but this is often where it shows up. After lovemaking, aura blending may present as a golden or white or shimmering cloud hanging around the room, emanating from both your and your partner's bodies. Sometimes, the room seems to glow with this light. If this happens to you, rejoice! It's a clear sign that you're in the right place with the right person! Aura blending also happens when a couple does deep spiritual practices together such as praying or meditating, or during some of the most intensive and beautiful moments of life on this earth: birthing a child, caring for another in illness, helping another transition into death.

Aura blending isn't a goal of a relationship; it's just something that can happen, and it's nice to see when it does. Think of it as an energetic rainbow between bodies, a visible show of the energy between you and another.

Symbiotic healing

Sometimes people in soul-mate relationships have an energetic connection so strong, they are able to shift, transform, or heal each other just by being in physical or mental proximity.

My client Rachel was always a flighty person, unsettled and unnerved by every little thing. When she met Tom, she felt as if someone had given her an extra dose of gravity. "He keeps me grounded," she told me. "I feel safe just being around him." Likewise Tom was elevated and lifted by Rachel's lighter, airy personality. Their particular energy filled in the gaps for each other; it was a symbiotic healing energy that healed them both.

If you and a partner experience symbiotic healing, you'll know it. Just being physically close to your partner will make you feel good, great, blissed out. Holding hands will send you over the moon, and you won't want to be away from him or her, even for one second.

Moreover, this snuggle-bunny stuff isn't just for teens or during the first stages of a new romance. Couples who experience symbiotic healing say that this physical sensation is constant throughout the relationship, lasting into old age.

Manifesting your soul mate

Manifesting (a.k.a. attracting) your soul mate is not particularly difficult. The only two parameters to determine before you do so are:

- Make sure you're clear. In other words, have you done all the work required to be fully detached from any previous relationships? For example, if you're married, you're not clear. If you're living with someone, you're not clear. If you've still got a photo of your old flame on the mantel, you're not clear. Before you manifest, get clear. (We'll talk more about getting clear in the next chapter.)

- Do you really want a soul mate at this particular time? I ask this, because even though love is a many-splendored thing, it's not for everyone, all the time. Soul mates are a lot of work. And maybe right now what you need is a break; you may need time for yourself. Maybe it's time for you to be by yourself. Maybe you're working on the *soul lesson* of experiencing yourself as an independent person right now, and that's the best possible lesson you can be working on. If you're not ready for a soul mate, he or she won't appear—the Universe simply won't product him/her. So be honest with yourself.

If, after looking into all of that, you decide you are indeed ready to attract your soul mate, simply do this exercise.

Exercise: Calling Your Beloved

If you are truly ready to call forth your soul mate, the Universe is ready to respond. There are many ways to do this, but for this particular exercise, we'll use writing. This allows you to take your time, put things down on paper, and keep that paper to review it later.

1. Find a quiet, private place to work.

2. Write down a list of all the qualities you'd like your soul mate to have. Make the list as long as you'd like. Have fun with this—write down everything that comes to mind.

3. Now, pare the list down to ten things. Yes, really! Even if your list was one hundred characteristics of "must haves," pare this list down to ten.

4. Now . . . drum roll, please . . . pare your list down to five things. I'm not kidding. By this time, you are getting to the core of what is truly, really, absolutely important. Now, your first list of five things might include something like this:

   - Looks like a supermodel
   - Multi millionaire
   - Drives an expensive car
   - Has a private jet
   - Hires a chef, maid, driver, personal trainer for me

   But . . . I'm more interested in seeing a list more along the lines of:

   - Reliable
   - Kind
   - Loves me
   - Wants a family
   - Has good friends

   or

   - Spiritual
   - Smart
   - Professional career
   - Loves my kids
   - Adores me

   or

   - Homebody
   - Loves family life

- Creative job
- Good sense of humor
- Open heart

Starting to get the picture? Now, if it's really, really, really important to you that your person has brown hair, brown eyes, and is six feet tall, or "no bald guys" or "bald guys only," then okay, I guess you can write that down.

But only if it's a deal-breaker.

Please remember you will be meeting a soul here—a soul that you already know, who simply happens to be dressed in a human body. Does it really matter what he/she looks like or any of the other smaller details? We're talking soul mate here! Why not leave the details up to the Universe, and be pleasantly surprised?

In any case:

1. Write these categories down—your top five.

2. Enter in, and spend a moment in meditation, asking the Universe to produce this person for you. Just ask it, in your mind.

3. Tuck your list in your wallet, dresser, or under your pillow—and then forget about it. Let the Universe do its thing. Relax, enjoy your life, don't worry about it.

4. When your soul mate arrives, drop me an email! I love to hear about soul mates meeting!

If you have yet to meet your Beloved, do not dismay.
What is required first is to open your heart into pain, into compassion,
into connection. When you have reached this place of opening,
your lover will appear.
—The Messages

---

sixteen

Healing from Love

Do not begrudge a past love. Thank him, thank her.
The lessons you have learned between you have moved you
further in your soul growth. In this way, you have gifted each other.

—The Messages

All that love stuff was great, wasn't it?

It's truly a gift to be with your Beloved, your soul mate, your other, in this lifetime.

But sometimes, as anyone over the age of fourteen knows, not all love lasts forever. And while that mushy, gushy love stuff feels over-the-moon great, blissed out, and blessed . . .

That "falling out of love" part?

Hmmm . . . not so much.

Unfortunately, the ending of a romantic relationship is no picnic in the park. Heartbreak, anguish, hopelessness, ennui—it's all fair game for a breakup. In fact, I'd personally rate relationship endings as pretty high on the Personal Pain & Suffering o-Meter! That's because when a love relationship ends, it just plain hurts.

187

Usually, the pain is in direct proportion to the duration and intensity of the relationship itself. The pain of being jilted after three minutes at a Speed Date event? Put a Band-Aid on it. The pain of breaking up after the most intensely connected summer of your life? You may need months to recover. The heartbreak of splitting up or divorcing after years in a committed relationship? It can sidetrack you for life.

Regardless of the ecstasy and agony involved, it happens.

One day you're "in love," the next, it's over.

Why does this happen, when at one time we were so intoxicated by our Beloved? How is this possible, when we were once so certain, so sure beyond shadow of a doubt, that our Beloved was our soul mate, true love, destiny?

Well, as you already know, he or she was.

That soul mate thing you experienced? It was true, real, complete, and whole.

It most definitely was "the real thing."

The problem is—we don't just have one *soul mate*.

We have myriad, multitudes, many. That whole "plenty of fish in the sea" concept? It's true. Of course, not all our soul mates are romantic soul mates—some are just the run-of-the-mill karmic crossings we experience all the time with family, friends, and colleagues.

Yet even if you narrow it down to those soul mates who are here to fulfill your romantic destiny—well, there's more than one. In your case, you may be so happy with the particular soul mate you meet at some time in your life that you don't have any need or desire to find another—you just blissfully live your life as a couple, until death do you part.

This is a wonderful situation!

But for most of us, at some point in a relationship, one of two things will happen:

1. The particular soul lessons you've been working on in a relationship are complete. Congratulations! You've learned them! Except, since the name of the life game is to keep learning soul lessons, it's time to move on to learn new lessons, by yourself or with

someone new. Like it or not, the Universe will make sure this happens.

2. The particular soul lessons you've been working on in a relationship are *not* complete—and, more importantly, it's become very clear that these lessons won't be learned in this lifetime. Staying in the relationship becomes redundant. It's just a rehash of the same old stuff, no learning at all. At that point, you need to pull the plug—or the Universe will do it for you.

When the lesson is complete, the necessity for the relationship is also complete. Such is the nature of karmic crossings. Such is the nature of soul growth.
—The Messages

Why love relationships end

It all sounds so harsh and unfeeling, but like it or not, it's how it works: once you've learned the soul lesson between you and another person, there's no need to linger. In fact, the Universe will make sure you don't, or can't, or won't.

Similarly, if you simply can't make any progress on your soul lessons with another person (he's a jerk, she's too stubborn, he won't listen, she's crazy, and so forth, with the exact same accusations being made about you!), the Universe will end the gig, cut bait—and move you into a new situation, where you can continue learning soul lessons.

No doubt about it, both completed or incomplete soul lessons (often disguised as "incompatibility" or "irreconcilable differences" or "betrayal" or "moving on") are always the energetic reason that people break up, split up, separate, and get divorced.

When soul lessons are complete, there's no hanging on, no trying to fan the ashes and get the fires burning again. It won't work. Neither will counseling sessions or couples therapy or a trip to Bali. When the karma is complete, the karma is complete. You can try all you want—you can cry all you want. But when the soul lessons are learned, they're learned. In these cases, people will split, separate, or divorce, and move quickly on to other relationships and/or other life lessons. Again, the Universe will help make this happen.

Similarly, when the soul lessons are stuck—when you've been working through kindergarten-level relationship stuff with your spouse or partner when by this time you both should be tackling college-level couples coursework—you'll also be asked to move on. The Universe is quite clear on this.

When karma is complete

When soul lessons are either complete or stuck between two people, the karmic connection naturally fizzles and is done. How to know if karma is complete? Some common characteristics include:

- The relationship feels flat.
- The relationship feels complete or "done."
- You can't see yourself with the person any longer.
- The person has nothing new to say to you, and vice versa.
- You aren't physically attracted to the person.
- Your energy feels incompatible.
- The physical aspects of the relationship don't interest you.
- Only the physical aspects of the relationship interest you.
- You don't really care.
- You see the person as an object or image rather than who they are.
- You see the person as a roommate, caretaker, friend—not a lover.
- You feel happy, independent, and free when you are not with the person.
- You feel confused, needy, angry, combative when you are with the person.
- You don't respect the person's life decisions.

- Your partner's habits drive you crazy.
- The relationship is centered around addictions, such as drugs, alcohol, cigarettes, food, shopping, trips, busyness, sex, the Internet, sports, media.
- The relationship is determined by status: career, physical looks, money, education, etc.
- One or both of you are obsessed with career or another interest; the relationship is secondary.
- One or both of you are deeply hooked in to your family, including children; the relationship is secondary.
- You live geographically apart most of the time.
- Even if you live in the same house, the bulk of your time is spent apart.
- You do not have clear, emotionally honest communication.
- One or both of you are not monogamous.

And, energetically speaking, there's likely more:

- You're not in vibrational match.
- You are heavily corded in unhealthy ways.
- You do not experience aura blending.
- You do not experience symbiotic healing.

Whew. Sounds like it's time to acknowledge the particular soul lessons for this relationship are complete, and make room for the Universe to bring you what is next.

How to heal from a broken relationship

Once you have determined a relationship is complete, it's time to move forward. This can be extraordinarily difficult. Sometimes, you don't think a relationship is finished, but your partner has decided it is. Or, you're the one who thinks a relationship is finished but your partner doesn't agree. Or, you both know you need to split—but you've got kids. Or, the dysfunction between you is so bad, you know the divorce or break is going to be even worse. And so on . . .

Ugh.

Ouch.

Yuck.

There's no ending that is not extremely difficult. Even if the divorce is "amicable" or if you tell everyone that "we're still good friends," after a breakup there's always underlying pain, anger, grief, heartbreak, deep hurt, loss—and these are just the run-of-the-mill feelings! Deluxe-edition emotions include rage, obsession, shame, depression, abandonment issues, suicidal thoughts, violence, and more.

If there are kids involved, divorce can be especially heartbreaking.

Sharon came to me to see about her eight-year relationship with her longtime boyfriend, Rupert. I immediately "saw" an image of ashes in a fireplace, the kind of damped-down ashes where it's impossible to get a flame going again, no matter how carefully you blow or stir or add tinder. An image like that has a clear symbolic meaning: this relationship was cold. As I looked into the energy of the relationship further, I saw clearly that Sharon was meant to be on her own for the next few years, not hooked in with this man. In this case, the highest possibility for Sharon was to release this relationship in love. As I provided this information to Sharon, she burst into tears. "I've know this for a long time," she confessed. "I just didn't want to admit it."

She and Rupert were able to look clearly at their relationship and see that what they really had was a friendship, not a romance. With that understood, they embarked on a supportive relationship that served them both beautifully—for this couple, at this stage, they were better friends than lovers. Their karmic crossing as lovers was complete, but as friends they were still not done.

In another case, Marta came to me because of her fifteen-year relationship with her boyfriend, Joe. She wanted out, but he wouldn't let her go. Joe was an alcoholic, and when he wasn't charming her, he was a kick-down-the-door drunk. "I've known him since my teens," she explained, "and when he's not drinking, he's a wonderful man." As Marta neared thirty, she realized that her true desire was to start a family—and Joe wasn't good father material. "What if he drank around the children?" she asked me, as tears ran down her face. Even though Marta saw the problem, she was afraid of stepping into the unknown. "But if I leave Joe, what if no one comes into my life, and I'm alone?" she worried. "What if I never have children?"

After much hard work and exploration, Marta realized that her dreams of family were well within her ability to create—but not with Joe. His addiction to alcohol was stronger than his love for her. She broke it off with him, and stepped with trepidation into the unknown. Within two weeks, she met a man at a work function—but she wasn't ready to date yet, she told him. It took him three months of asking before she finally went out with him for coffee. "The minute I stepped into the coffee shop, I knew I'd made the right decision," she said. The new man, Brandon, was looking for long-term commitment—he was ready to start a family, no alcohol required. "If I'd never had the courage to break with Joe, I'd have never met Brandon," she acknowledged.

In another situation, Michaela had been married to Jeremy for six years, and they had two young daughters. "I feel like I can't trust him," she told me at our first meeting, and when I looked intuitively into the situation, I saw indeed that she couldn't—he had a heavy addiction to gambling. In fact, the gambling was threatening to unhinge the family's financial structure. At first, when I told her there wasn't another woman, Michaela disagreed. "I'm positive there's someone else," she said. But as we worked further, Michaela began to understand that "the other woman" wasn't a flesh-and-blood woman—it was the addiction itself. At this time, the Universe was asking her if she valued herself enough to live this way; the soul lesson at this time was self-worth.

The ties that bind

Okay, so you've figured out that your soul lessons with your spouse, partner, boyfriend, or girlfriend are complete. Or, you understand suddenly, in a flash of recognition, that they will never be complete in this lifetime. You and/or the Universe have come to the sad truth that it's time to separate. You know in your heart that this is true. And you know it's not going to be easy—it's never easy.

Maybe you're the one who leaves. Maybe your partner decides to split from you. In any case, you break up. It's the worst heartbreak you've ever experienced in your life. But you do it anyway.

And, after an appropriate time of grieving the relationship (any-where from one hour to a lifetime), you finally feel ready to move for-ward. You fall in love again, and you enter into a new life with this new person. You know this person is fantastic for you! You know this person is your soul mate, true love, destiny.

And he or she is.

The trouble is, you can't get your old love out of your head.

And not in a good way either—but in an obsessive, snaky, unhealthy way, such as Googling him/her, Facebook-stalking, rereading old texts and emails, and looking at pictures of you together three years ago on the beaches of Maui.

Sigh.

Or maybe you've worked really hard to get that person out of your life, out of your head. But he/she won't leave you alone: you see a famil-iar car parked across from your apartment in the wee hours of morning. Your phone gets mysterious hang-ups from blocked numbers. You hear from friends that he/she's been asking about you.

Or perhaps it's even more complicated. Perhaps because you have kids, you're stuck co-parenting for the next fifteen years, and you realize that you will see your ex at every single youth soccer game that you will be attending for the next decade and a half.

Can you say awkward?

Sigh.

All of this happens, because even though your karmic lessons are complete (or won't be completed in this lifetime), your energetic cord-ing is still attached.

And this, dear reader, is definitely something you can do something about.

Exercises

There are a few exercises that can help you release energetic ties to another person. This will be of great benefit to you and will help you to be calmer in this person's presence, stop obsessively thinking about him or her, and stop him or her from obsessively thinking about you.

Doing these exercises, either one or all, will shift things quickly. Sometimes it is necessary to do them a few times if the karmic cording is very deep and the relationship has been important and long-term, such as in a marriage or a longtime partnership.

Releasing Past Loves

1. Sequester yourself in a quiet, private place.

2. Write down the names of every person you've been involved with romantically. You can do this chronologically, or you can do this simply as each person arrives into your consciousness. You may be surprised by who shows up first!

3. Close your eyes, bring in a guide, and connect with each person telepathically, asking them what soul lesson you learned together.

4. Write down what soul lessons you have learned from each person on your list. Now, spend some time journaling on each person, writing whatever comes to mind until you are complete.

5. Over the next few days, see what new understanding occurs. For example, if during all your adult relationships your soul lesson has been rebellion, then this is a pattern that would give pause. Surely, by the time you are an adult, you do not need to use your love life as an act of rebellion. Or perhaps you do. With illumination comes understanding.

Clearing Cording

Even if relationships are over, the energetic cording can remain. In fact, it usually does. You can review how to remove these energy cords in chapter 13. Begin to do a session of clearing karmic cording from or to the person you were in romantic relationship with. Don't be shocked if the karmic cording is thick, full, and strong—so thick you may need to get a hacksaw or chainsaw (energetic!) to cut through it. Don't be surprised if this karmic cording goes through your heart, or twines throughout your entire body. Sometimes the other person can still energetically inhabit your own energetic body. If you really get stuck, ask your spirit guides and angels to come in and remove the cording for you. You will be amazed at how many cords there are, how thick and tightly wrapped they are, and how your guides are effortlessly able to remove them from you.

When your guides are finished, say thank you. Notice how much lighter and brighter you feel.

Releasing via Ritual
Ritual is one of the most intensive ways to release energetic ties from the past—it works emotionally, symbolically, and energetically, and may be done as often as needed.

1. Choose a day when you are ready to release your energetic entanglements with this other person. Mark this day on your calendar.

2. In preparation, collect objects that have meaning for you surrounding this relationship. These could be letters, photos, wedding rings, gifts—anything that represents this relationship to you.

3. On the day of the releasing ritual, head out to a location where you can be alone, such as in nature. If nature isn't available to you easily, a quiet spot at home will do.

4. This day is between you and the other person, so you won't want anyone else to come along. This extends to the time after the ritual is over—it's a sacred matter, not to be discussed at large with friends, family, or the Facebook community. It's for you to experience in a private, discreet way.

5. Burn, bury, shred, or toss the items (local ordinances permitting!) that you have collected. For example, you might start a small campfire on a deserted beach and burn the letters the other person wrote you. You might throw a wedding ring into the ocean. You could shred some photos and bury them in the earth at the base of a big oak tree. Remember: ritual is energetic, symbolic, emotional. Allow yourself to feel what you feel.

6. Watch the smoke drift, the waves lap, the earth cover. Watch and realize that all things are temporal experiences. Understand that this relationship was a necessary part of your soul growth. If you have completed karma with this person, be thankful. If you were not able to complete karma with this person, understand that you will meet him or her in a next lifetime, and have the chance to try again.

7. Give thanks for what you have learned, or what you have failed to learn. Understand that this lifetime is a gift, in all its experiences.

Each stage of life brings with it lessons suitable for this stage: the child, the adolescent, the multiple passages of adult life. Do not tarry in the past. Allow yourself to move forward, when the next lesson arrives.

—The Messages

Part Five

———— ❧ ————

Beyond Time
& Space

seventeen

Past-Life Regression

You have known from your first breath, and you will know beyond your last breath. This is the nature of Divine information.
—The Messages

Most people get excited about the idea of experiencing a past-life regression, sure that they'll discover something marvelous about themselves that will make everything fall into place. And they probably will.

However, as a caveat, this may or may not include a past life in which:

- You were Cleopatra
- You ruled Atlantis
- You were King Tut's personal headwear assistant
- You were one of Jesus's apostles
- You were Elvis (skinny version)

I provide this disclaimer, because sometimes a certain kind of disingenuous psychic practitioner or regression therapist will inform a naive client (certainly not you!) that he or she had what I would call a "celebrity" past life as Elvis or someone named Matthew, Mark, Luke, or John.

Of course we all want to hear fantastic things about ourselves! We all want people who "see things" to say they see wonderful things about us! But whether or not these things are valid or viable is another story.

So be cautious. Be skeptical. Don't let your ego believe what your heart isn't sure about. My first rule of thumb to avoid getting into this kind of situation is: don't let a psychic, hypnotist, therapist (or anyone else!) tell you who you were in a past life.

Instead, have him or her take you through a proper past-life regression process, so you can experience one of these lifetimes yourself. Yes, it takes more time; yes, it's more work; but it's infinitely more accurate. It's also infinitely more meaningful—going there, and seeing, feeling, and existing for a moment in that lifetime rather than just having someone tell you their version.

And while you're there in that state of regression, be curious. Keep your expectations open. Stay humble. Ego shut, heart open! It is really not necessary for your personal soul growth that you previously existed as Cleopatra or Elvis. It's just not.

In fact, from what I've seen, most people don't have particularly "celebrity" past lives at all.

Oh sure, you've probably got a handful of super-duper-exciting past lives somewhere in your history—maybe you were once a pirate or an explorer. Who knows? You probably also have some fairly tragic past lives in the mix—lifetimes in which you were killed, fell ill, died in childbirth, and so on.

But from what I have seen with my clients, the majority of experiences are not champagne-and-caviar lifetimes. Instead, they're quite ordinary, everyday kinds of lifetimes in which we exist simply as farmer, peasant, mother, father, child, and so forth and so on.

Not particularly hothouse flowers.

But in terms of soul growth, learning and growing like weeds.

One of my favorite past-life experiences was with my client Jenna, a person who'd had a very conservative upbringing, in a family that was 100 percent teetotaller. To Jenna's family, alcohol was the devil's brew.

Imagine her surprise when her first past-life regression led her immediately to a boisterous German pub—in which she experienced herself as very drunken young man in lederhosen, beer stein firmly in hand!

Chicken dance, anyone?

Humble, simple, or everyday lives are just as valuable as over-the-top celebrity lifetimes. That's because even the most mundane life is loaded with opportunities to learn soul lessons and to expand our human hearts. Each lifetime, no mater how big or small, is of crucial importance to our soul growth.

But I'm getting ahead of myself with all these cautions and disclaimers. Let's start from the beginning.

All lifetimes, perceptions, thoughts, realities exist as One.
Thus, it is the simplest thing to experience another lifetime,
in linear aspect of past or future.
Merely close your eyes, and you are there.
—The Messages

A continuum of lifetimes

Each of us experiences a continuum of lifetimes that extend back into the past, forward into the future, and include this present one. I don't know how many lifetimes we get—some people believe there's an infinite amount, some think there's a finite number. Is that number 47? 593? 2,701,602? I really don't know, and I'm taking bets that no one else does either.

Really, most of life is pure mystery.

In my own practice, I help clients experience past-life regression, and from what I have seen it's clear that most of us have access to what appears to be an unlimited number of past lives. Most folks can experience at least one or sometimes two past lives in a session. Yet even though time constraints or exhaustion ends the session there, it seems to me that are always more past lives, waiting to be explored.

That said, we're here to live in the present. The importance of past lives is not in tallying how many we've had. Instead, it's the content each life contains. That's because without exception, every past life holds pertinent information, patterns, and emotional information that are useful to you in this present lifetime.

If you faced a certain soul lesson then, and you're facing it again now, then that's good information to have. Perhaps, in this lifetime, by knowing what this soul lesson is, you can make more progress!

One of my clients, Dianne, was a plucky, self-sufficient woman who longed to meet her soul mate—but he had not appeared. At forty-seven, she'd already missed the biological window of opportunity for childbearing, and now she wondered if she'd ever find the companionship, love, and true partnering she'd always dreamed of.

Her first past-life regression came spontaneously during a clairvoyance workshop I was teaching; the rest of the students sat stunned as Dianne reported what she was seeing in trance: herself as a girl running away from a restrictive Victorian home, and stowing away on a boat as it left to sail from England to America. On the ship she met her soul mate, who asked her, "Where have you been all this time?" The two spent every waking moment together during the rest of the voyage— but then tragedy struck. On a stormy night, she watched her lover get washed overboard, and then she herself drowned.

Ugh.

"Was that me?" Dianne asked, coming out of trance, as the rest of the class leaned forward in their chairs, wanting to hear more. "I've never felt or experienced anything like that before. It was like a dream, but it was so real. I knew everything about that place and time."

Because energetically, of course, she'd been there.

Intrigued, she began to work with me privately, and during one of our training sessions, we did another past-life regression (this time a planned one!). In this regression, Dianne found herself in a medieval village somewhere in northern Europe, again as a girl. This time she was bound by the restraints of her father, who kept her close to the house. At a village celebration, she met a man who again said to her something along the lines of "Where were you?" She agreed to meet him secretly, and the next day ran away from the village to be with him. This time there was no tragic drowning—the two married and lived quite happily in a neighboring town, although they never had children.

In asking Dianne to take a look at the symbolic and emotional meaning that particular lifetime contained, a few things surfaced. In both of these lifetimes, she'd been initially restricted by an authority figure who didn't want her to leave, explore, or go anywhere. In both lifetimes, she'd gone anyway. Both times, she met a man who instantly recognized her. In one lifetime, they had scant time together; in the other, many years. She didn't have children in either lifetime.

Now, these are just two of Dianne's past lives. There are many more that she could look at. However, in most cases, I've found that the past life that presents in a regression is most often the experience that will be most beneficial to you.

In Dianne's case, her particular past-life experiences didn't make sense at first. "I don't have anyone controlling me in this lifetime," she stated. But as she delved deeper, she realized that it wasn't a person who was controlling her in this lifetime—it was her job. For years she'd worked for a top international corporation. And because everything is energy, and everything works energetically, a corporation or an employer is also an energetic entity, with its own characteristics, personality, and vibration.

Yep, you got it—energetically, a corporation can behave just like a person.

In this case, the corporation she worked for was playing the role of the Victorian parents, or the restrictive father. Dianne had long wanted to quit her job with the company and start her own business, but she'd been afraid to leave the security it represented. "Nobody quits the kind of job I have," she said. "It's safe and secure."

It was also mind-numbing, spirit-killing, and not what Dianne was supposed to be doing with her life. But her fear of leaving "security" had her stuck. In exploring these two past lives, it became clear that in this lifetime, her soul lesson was that she must once again escape the forces that were controlling and restricting her.

Interestingly, the day she gave her notice, she told me she felt an overwhelming sense of freedom. "I knew this feeling. I'd felt it before," she said. "It was the same feeling I experienced when I jumped on ship, or when I snuck off from the village."

At the time of this writing, Dianne's adventure hasn't unfolded long enough for her to have met a partner who will ask her, "Where were you, anyway?" But from my own visioning, I'm confident that the Universe is busy arranging this exact scenario.

Entering the Now

Much of past-life regression work is done by hypnotists, who take people into a deep hypnotic state. In my own work, I use a light level of trance—the same level that we've used already in clairvoyant work, in channeling or channeled writing, in meeting guides and angels, and in mediumship.

No doubt about it, it's a "sweet spot" for Universal information!

However, even though we journey to the same layer or level as we do for other intuitive activities, a regression experience often *feels* more intense than a clairvoyant journey, or even a visit with your spirit guides and angels.

That's because a regression experience often presents as more fully dimensional—you can see, hear, smell, and experience things as if you were there, because, in fact, you are there.

As you know, all time and space is infinitely connected. It doesn't exist in a linear fashion at all. Layers or levels of consciousness exist simultaneously. Space isn't near or far away—it's all around us, at all times. Time isn't in the past or in the future—it's happening concurrently, everything at the same time.

What's that? you're saying.

That booked calendar on my smartphone means squat?

That schedule I'm a slave to doesn't really exist?

That GPS I use to get me from one place to another isn't needed?

Well, yes. And no.

Because even though time, space, and consciousness are operating simultaneously in the Now, the world we live in is pretty set on clocks and calendars! Sure it's an illusion—but it's how the earth world works.

However, energetically, whether you're awake or meditating or dreaming—it's all the same stuff. To the Universe, what happens in your room, or in another country, or on another planet—it's all the same stuff. To the Universe, what happened three years ago, three hundred years ago, three thousand years ago—it's all the same stuff.

Which makes it very easy for us to *jump levels*.

Jumping levels

You know the DeLorean? That time machine/car that they used in the movie *Back to the Future*? Or how about the hot tub that served as a time portal in the flick *Hot Tub Time Machine*? (Please, let's refrain from commenting about the types of movies I watch!) Well, those are silly movies—but what's fun about them is that, on some level, they illustrate how easy it is to move energetically back and forward in time.

Except, no car or hot tub required!

In the DeLorean, there was some kind of gauge to determine where you would end up—which year of the past you were driving to. The Hot Tub Time Machine also had some kind of gauge.

In past-life regression, however, such a gauge doesn't exist.

That means, when you enter in to a past life, you commit to moving into the mystery, having no idea what lies ahead. You don't know what's around the next corner; you don't know who you'll meet; you don't know what events will happen in this past time frame.

This is why it is so important to set an intention, or create a container for the experience you want to have. I offer this advice from experience. Use it or ignore it, but don't say I didn't warn you!

When I first started experimenting with past-life regression, I didn't bother to create a container for my experience. When it comes to this kind of psychic stuff, I'm a risk taker—I'll often leap without a net. My attitude's often been "That sounds like fun! I'll give it a try! What could possibly go wrong?"

Oops.

Thus, without taking proper precautions, without setting intention, without asking my guides to accompany me, without even donning a helmet, which at least Dr. Brown had the foresight to do in *Back to the Future*, I headed willy-nilly back into whatever past-life experience I'd find.

Ahem. Bad idea.

On the first regression I attempted, I discover myself as a young girl of about eight, trapped in an upstairs room of an old-style European house—complete with criss-cross wood on the outer walls and a beamed ceiling. It's nearly dusk, and buildings are on fire throughout the town; smoke chokes the air. My house will be engulfed in flames soon. No one is here with me—my family's gone. I understand I'd had a baby brother or sister, a mother and father; I know my older brother and grandmother have died. I want to scream and cry, but I don't dare—just a few houses away, a militia is rampaging, dragging people out of their homes and killing them. In a few moments, they'll be here. I race down narrow stairs—they're worn in the middle, bowed. I flee across the cobbled street, and a group of men set chase, but somehow I escape into the smoke. I run into a forest, which I know is the Black Forest—it's the place we've been warned never to go. I huddle against a tree as darkness falls. I can hear screaming from the village, and see the flames. I am cold, terrorized, heartbroken, and after a few days, I die. I experience this pain fully during my regression. When I come out of this experience, it takes me two days to recover.

You'd think, at this point, I'd have figured out a better way.

But, intrepid explorer that I am, I try another one a few weeks later. This time, the experience is even worse.

On my second regression, I'm a girl again, but older—maybe fourteen or fifteen. I'm upstairs in a building in Europe, hidden away from the Nazis, just like Anne Frank. But I'm not in Amsterdam—I think I'm in France. I'm not in a city either—I'm by myself, in an old farmhouse where I have been hidden away by an older woman and her husband. Once again, the rest of my family is gone. When the Nazis come through, there is a secret floor space that I hide in. I experience myself lying down flat in the space between the actual floor and what is a fake floor, for hours. I don't experience my death in this regression, but I feel fully the terror of the hiding, and the intense loneliness.

After that regression, I decided to take a new approach, and not just hurtle myself into random past lives filled with militias and/or Nazis! Instead, I decided (as I should have in the first place) that I was going to let the Divine lead. That I would ask my spirit guides and angels to drive my particular DeLorean. And that I'd set a container or boundary, so that the past lives that I viewed (a) were not violent, (b) were not painful, and (c) clearly showed the pattern or soul lesson that I was working on this lifetime, as well.

Wow! What an improvement!

The next times I entered in, I experienced:

- A lovely life as an ancient Chinese healer. I was an older woman and lived in the household of a patron—a large farmhouse filled with children and relatives, none of them mine. I had a long table and giant chests with tiny drawers, and I sorted herbs and did hands-healing for the people in the area—they waited in line to see me. I was literate—I saw myself writing. I was revered by the villagers, and thus considered dangerous to the ruling political system. One day on a trip to the forest to collect herbs, a soldier came to me and chopped off my head with a sword. However, because I had asked to have this experience excluded, I felt nothing—no pain or fear; I just knew that was the end of that life. That lifetime was pleasant, useful, and enjoyable. This regression was meant to show me the lesson of being on my life's path, which in that lifetime was healing.

    A few days after that regression, I was in Portland and stopped in at a Chinese antique store. Way in the back there was an ancient medicine chest with multiple drawers—the same kind that I'd seen in my regression. The sense of familiarity was so strong I nearly collapsed; in touching the chest, I felt a strong sense of "This was once mine." And, as these things tend to work out, perhaps it once was.

- In another regression, I'm also on my life's path. I am a medieval monk, and my job is as scribe—I copy down sacred texts all day long. I'm sitting at a slanted table, writing. I write from dawn to dusk, until my back goes stiff. I am young, just in my twenties, but my body feels old from sitting so long. There is bliss in the room, a Divine infusion. There is also unrest in the church, and I am mistakenly considered a heretic, or blasphemous. I am taken out and hanged one day, but during this regression I have no fear, no pain—I just enjoy the feeling of connection to the Divine.

This regression was meant to show me the lesson of being a writer, and of being connected with the Divine. It also showed me that even back then, sitting for long hours as a writer can make your back hurt!

And so on. Every time I enter in, a different past life appears, or I am shown a more complete aspect of one these past lives above—the experience extends and expands for further understanding.

Finally, although I do plenty of past-life regression with clients, I don't spend a lot of time looking back anymore. No doubt about it; I have been informed deeply by these explorations. But after looking at so many of them, it seems that the best place to be—in fact the only place—is right here, right now, attending to the relationships and tasks in front of me.

Exercise: Entering a Past Life

If you are working with a partner, ask your partner to "talk you in" as you do the exercise and ask you questions about what you are experiencing once you have reached your destination. If you're working alone, just experience what happens.

1. Do your setup, as described on page 13.

2. Go up three levels of vibration to the place where it's easiest for you to receive psychic and spiritual information.

3. Ask a guide or angel to appear, in order to accompany you.

4. Think back to a time period earlier today, and review it in your mind. Where were you? What were you doing? Re-experience this time period.

5. Next, go back to a time period yesterday. Recall and re-experience what you were doing then. For example, you may find yourself at the breakfast table, drinking coffee. Notice the color and shape of the coffee cup. Notice something or someone else in the room.

6. Go back to a time period one week ago. Just let any experience from last week float up into your consciousness. Recall it in detail.

7. Go back to an experience three months ago. Don't worry about specific dates or events. Simply experience whatever comes to mind.

8. Now, we will start moving backward at a faster pace; as soon as your mind has tracked on an experience, go back further. Go back to an experience one year ago.

9. Go back to an experience five years ago.

10. When you were twenty-six. (If you are not yet twenty-six, just skip to the next one.)

11. When you were eighteen.

12. When you were twelve.

13. When you were seven.

14. When you were two. Imagine yourself seeing things from a toddler's point of view, and notice what you see.

15. When you were an infant. Again, imagine yourself in the infant's mind, and notice what you see.

16. When you were in your mother's womb. Feel the heat, rhythm, and comfort of this place.

17. When you were conceived. Allow yourself to experience what this was like.

18. Now, your guide will show you a tunnel or walkway, in which you will be walking forward toward a dim light that gradually

becomes brighter. Notice the walls—are they smooth, rocky, or something else? Begin walking toward the light at the end of this walkway. As you walk toward this light, you will begin to see a doorway or portal, and you will realize that once you walk through this doorway, you will find yourself in a past life.

19. Walk through the doorway, and notice where you find yourself. Become aware of your surroundings.

20. Look down at your hands, and notice if you have the hands of a man or woman, young or old person. Feel the cloth or clothing you are wearing, if any. Is it scratchy, smooth, poor, rich? Look at the color of your skin. Feel your hair, and determine what kind of hair you have, if any. Allow yourself to recognize your identity through deep knowing, such as "I am a male monk of about twenty years old, living in France," or "I am a boy of about nine, living in colonial America." It will be easy for you to recognize yourself, and to know your identity.

21. From this point, head toward whatever catches your attention. If a person is in your area of viewing, go to that person and see who they are, and what they'd like to tell you. If there's a building, go there. Allow yourself to be drawn to what you need to experience, always asking, "Tell me more" or "Show me more" if the vision stops expanding.

22. If you find yourself in any sticky situations, or don't know what to do next, simply turn to your guide and ask for help.

23. Allow yourself to feel the emotions of this past life deeply and fully. Embedded in the emotions of this experience will be further information.

24. When you have experienced enough of this past life, and it seems complete, simply tell your guide you would like to return to your present life.

25. You will immediately see yourself being whisked from the past to this present life. This can go very fast sometimes, so hang on!

26. Find yourself back in your body, count yourself back in to present reality, and open your eyes.

27. Now is an excellent time to journal about your experience. As a word of caution, it is best not to talk about your experience with others too quickly, until you have had time to consider the soul lessons that this past life contains.

As a soul, you learn lessons in continuum over last lifetime, this lifetime, next lifetime. If you are able to recognize the lesson, it is near completion. Look now; know what you see!

—The Messages

eighteen

Energy Healing

When you heal another, you also heal yourself.
Know this clearly: you are not separate from another;
you are both the same. What affects one, affects all.
—The Messages

For months I'd been having pain on my right side. The area was tender to the touch, and I knew something was wrong. Yet a visit to my physician didn't turn up anything wrong—so I resigned myself to this strange persistent pain.

Shortly after my checkup, I was spending time with a few energy-healer friends, and one offered to do some energy work on me. Not expecting anything but always ready for good energy, I said, "Sure" and jumped on her table.

Almost immediately her hands found the area where my pain was. "This feels hot," she said, hovering her hands over my right side as she began to work energetically. I quickly fell into deep trance, traveling across many dimensions so quickly I nearly passed out—and I soon knew why. I suddenly felt the presence of angels: tall, pale, winged, who bent over me, and then, how can I explain this . . . they opened up my side.

It was painless, but there was a pulling or a pressure—the way it feels getting stitches if you are anesthetized but still awake. The angels proceeded to "cut" into the organ and snip some of it away; the organ felt pulpy and swollen, but it didn't hurt. They next began to sew up the organ; it was much smaller at this point! Again, no pain, but tugging and pressure—I definitely could tell what they were doing. The entire process took only a few minutes, during which the practitioner never physically touched me.

When the angels were done working on me, the healer sensed it—she soon ended the session. I got up from the table stunned by what had happened. My side felt entirely healed, and, in fact, I've never had any trouble with it since; the problem has simply disappeared.

Does energy healing work?

Does energy healing work? I wasn't sure, until I had the miraculous experience above—and subsequently began to experience similar healings with energy healers using all kinds of techniques: Reiki, Matrix Energetics, the Reconnection, you name it. With each healing, it became clear to me that even though we don't fully understand how energy healing works, from what I have experienced in my own body—it just does.

Others are starting to agree—and not just New Agers, but a whole slew of mainstream experts and authors. For example, *O: The Oprah Magazine* recently ran a full-length feature on John of God of Brazil, considered by many to be a miracle healer. Top authors such as Bernie Siegel, M.D., posit that people can think themselves to health; renowned authors Dr. Mona Lisa Schulz and Carolyn Myss both call themselves medical intuitives.

My feeling is that we are only at the beginning of understanding how healing works. Certainly, we're further along than a hundred years ago, or even a few years back. Still, we have a long way to go. As we explore further in all the modalities—traditional, holistic, energetic, spiritual—we will gain a better understanding of how these methods fit together and complement each other.

Approaches to healing

I know a lot of healers, and I am intrigued by the different ways they work. Different modalities flourish, and it is interesting to see who studies what, who uses what.

Some of you heal with your hands, some with your minds, and some in other ways. We all have unique gifts in this area, meant for unique purposes. And usually, it's very easy to tell what method of healing is going to work best for you.

For example, many of you out there are hands healers—if we were in session together, I could hold your hands and instantly know that this was your calling, your life's path. I find there's a particular sort of density in the hands of a hands healer that is unique to this type of person. The hands feel grounded, calm, capable. It doesn't matter if the hands are big or small; what matters is the density.

For example, my partner is a chiropractor and a hands healer—his hands feel like the earth: solid, broad, warm. A massage therapist I know also has hands that feel the same way. If you're a hands healer, you probably already know it—chances are good that you're already working in or thinking about working in the healing fields. You may be a chiropractor, massage therapist, or any of the other healing professions that work both with anatomy and energy. But many of you are energy healers who won't use your hands as a primary tool of healing.

Instead, you'll use your minds.

If you are this kind of person, you'll have a different density to your hands than a hands healer. For example, my own hands are lighter, less dense, almost airy. Most of the people I know who are intuitives also have a lighter density in their hands that is similar to mine.

Other folks have even different energy densities—such as the vibrational density of people who are able to grow plants, work with animals, play music, perform surgery, deliver babies, and so on. I once held the hands of a gifted arborist; her hands felt like a tree—I don't know how to explain it, but there it was.

Just by holding the hands of a person, you can know all about their energy, their vibration, and the type of healing they will be best at. Try it now! Ask someone to hold your hands and tell you what they feel. Hold someone else's hands, or a few different people's, and notice the differences and similarities.

If you are a hands healer, people will tell you your hands are warm, sturdy, capable, solid. You may also find your hands have an "itch" to heal something. If you're more of a mind healer, your hands will feel less dense, lighter. If you are another type of healer, you will feel called to your own particular area.

The Universe, all energy, seeks continually to flow.
When you work in energy, you become a point of conduit for flow;
this is within your capabilities now.
—The Messages

Healing with the mind

Healing with the mind is not particularly hard, especially since you've been reading and working in this book. Thus, you already know how to:

- Sense energy in people, places, and objects
- Enter in to other layers and levels
- Shift energy, such as turning your body from "green" to "orange" to "white"
- Match your vibration to other people/objects
- Communicate with spirit guides and/or the departed
- Receive symbolic and embedded emotional meaning from guides, saints, Holy Ones, and/or the departed
- Heal relationships in the present
- Heal relationships in the past and future
- Experience past lives

Once you know how to do these things, it makes it very easy to turn your brain to healing tasks, and learn how to:

- Sense illness via medical intuition
- Heal through vibrational matching
- Heal through spirit guides
- Heal through heart's opening

Sensing illness via medical intuition

If you've been to a medical intuitive, you may have been stunned at the level of specific detail that this person told you about what's happening in your body. Basically, a medical intuitive reads or senses the body, either in person or from a distance, and then tells you what areas of the body are ill or need attention. Medical intuitives who know how to recognize anatomy and body systems will be able to "see" and recognize specific aspects, and perhaps even name particular diseases.

However, even if you don't have a clear understanding of anatomy (saaaay, is that my liver or my left elbow?), you can still sense illness in the body.

Remember, all is energy. What you are looking for in medical intuition follows from the old *Sesame Street* saying: "One of these things is not like the other; one of these things just doesn't belong." Simply by energetically scanning the body, you can look for areas of difference. Usually, areas that are injured, ill, diseased, or stressed present with different energetic density or color than the rest of the body.

Going back to sensing, as we did in chapter 5, you can imagine that your body is vibrating at a certain level, and that it is common to see this level as a color. Check now, gauge which color you are vibrating at. In working with the body, the colors that most frequently present are the colors we associate with the chakras, or energy centers in Eastern spirituality, which range from lower or deeper vibration to lighter and higher vibration. These usually are:

- Red
- Orange

- Yellow

- Green

- Blue

- Purple

- White

You may also see other colors besides those listed above—I personally vibrate at hot pink most of the time, and almost never at yellow. That's just how I vibrate, I guess. You'll also vibrate differently at different times of day, on different days, depending on how you feel, what you're doing, and who you're spending time with. I have clients who most often find themselves at green or blue; others are consistently at purple; and some hang out in orange and red a lot.

Remember: each color is simply a level of vibration—no color is better than another. It just is what it is, the same as no musical note is better than another—they are just different.

In any case, check in with your body now, and see what color you're vibrating at. Let's say you're a green. Sense all the green, everywhere in your body—and then look carefully, as if you're doing a body scan (no, not the airport kind, a psychic one!), and notice if there are any areas of your body that are not vibrating green. Look especially for denser, darker colors, or "angry" colors. Often, illness in the body shows up as:

- A difference in density

- Grayness

- Blackness

- Angry red, such as fiery or flames

- Other ways of showing a "no match" in vibrational alignment, such as swelling, hotness, coldness, pulsing, wateriness, and so forth

When you intuitively scan a person's body energy, you can look for this type of "no match" by sensing areas of difference in color or density. If you spot an area of difference, explore it further and see what it tells you. Here are some examples of how I approach this process:

- Linda, in her early seventies, came to me for a reading, and asked if I saw any health issues for her. Before I could even begin to scan Linda's body energetically, I immediately saw a roadwork of blue in my mind's eye. Looking closer, I perceived an entire network of blood-filled veins, like a road map. Because I don't have medical training, I'm not able to identify these veins in a specific way, such as "Those are leg veins" or "Those are chest veins." To me, they just look like veins. For whatever reason, I sensed that the vein issues surrounded Linda's legs. Energetically, her legs seemed slow, throbbing. Worse, there appeared to be a pulsing red, and then a tenderness that was gray and swollen. Normally, a healthy body doesn't pulse red, and gray is usually a bad sign. I advised her to see her doctor as soon as she could. Sure enough, her doctor reported that she had developed a vein condition that can be associated with blood clots.

- During an intuitive training session, Karen kept rubbing her neck and wincing. As I scanned her energetically, I saw that she was vibrating red—a color that surrounds family, security, survival, and sex. Her neck especially was vibrating a deep, angry, blood-colored red—darker than the rest of her body. This color extended from her neck all the way into her heart and chest. As I looked further, a vision of an older woman came into my mind's eye—she was grouchy, and sitting stiffly in a chair. When I mentioned the woman, Karen revealed that her mother had recently had surgery, and Karen had been taking care of her round-the-clock for the last few weeks. She broke into tears and confessed that she felt guilty that her mother's surgery was "a pain in the neck" for her, but she found it hard to handle with her job and family. The moment she said this, the angry red dissolved, and I understood that this emotional release would be healing for her.

- Brett was a skinny, high-energy man in his forties. The problem was, even though he had a lot of energy, he couldn't seem to harness it. As CEO of his own company, he was always on the go—and while working, he enjoyed his nonstop ability to make things happen. The trouble came whenever he had to wait, slow down, stay at home or in a hotel, or even sleep. As I scanned him energetically, I noticed his color was a fiery orange. Yet to my concern, his heart was pulsing at high violet—and as I looked further, I saw a vision of his heart turning black and shrinking to the size of a walnut, then smaller still. I understood instantly that unless Brett learned some methods of stabilizing his energy, he was going to have a heart attack in the next few years. He listened, and although he was never able to sit still long enough to meditate, he began a regular program of running—this helped him release the adrenaline that he was so used to "running" on.

Healing through vibrational matching

Once you know how to scan the body and sense the areas of difference, you can explore further. As you enter in to look more closely, you may receive clairvoyant visions or clairaudient messaging about the situation, as in the above examples—I saw or was told the health problem would get worse if proper care (doctor, change of lifestyle, etc.) wasn't acquired.

However, sometimes you can adjust, align, or attune the energy right there on the spot, by creating vibrational matching in the body. Just as you easily turned your own body from orange to blue to white in chapter 5, so too can you turn the vibrational level or color in another person's body from one level or color to another. For example:

Judy came to me with a dazzling purple energy; a gifted clairvoyant, she lived with her mind in the ethers most of the time. Unfortunately, this lack of grounding was creating practical problems with her finances and health. She had plenty of money, but she couldn't remember to pay her bills. Or, she'd go to the store and pick up a new crystal—but forget to pick up milk and bread. She couldn't be bothered to eat regularly, and this made her tired and unable to focus.

As I scanned her body, I saw that she wasn't ill yet, but her energy was out of alignment—not all areas of her body were vibrating the same. Most of her body vibrated purple, but in the areas of the stomach, there was a density difference—almost as if a piece of her was missing there. I took her into a light trance, and had her imagine that the purple color that filled most of her body would now completely fill her stomach area—there would be no "empty" place. She reported a feeling of warmth coming into her stomach immediately, like a warm rush in her organs.

More grounding was needed, so over the next month I directed her to take some time off of intuitive realm activities, and get organized: pay bills, stock up on groceries, take out the trash, go for a walk. Earth life stuff. She soon reported that she felt stronger and more focused—and best of all, she had an appetite for the first time in years.

If a person is unable to enter in to assist with their own vibrational matching, you can do this for them, either in person or from a distance. Simply call up the person into your mind's eye, and notice what vibrational level most of their body is at—again, this usually presents as a color. Then, notice any areas of density, grayness, blackness, and so forth—any areas that look different. When you discover an area of difference, simply ask that energy to shift to match the main vibrational color. Again, you're going to request this of the energy. You're not doing anything. You're just asking that it be done.

If the energy is unable to shift, take that as a clear message that it's time to see a doctor, either medical or holistic.

If the energy shifts easily, you will know it—it will shift gloriously and beautifully, and the energy body will be flooded with one vibrational color. Energetically, this is where healing begins. It is always prudent to seek medical care, but energy healing is a great complement to traditional methods.

Healing through spirit guides

As humans, we can be pretty decent healers. But when it comes to the tough cases, it makes sense to call in the experts—the spirit guides, saints, and Holy Ones who live and work in Divine energy, day in and day out. We've all heard of the power of prayer to heal; the stories of angels and other entities doing miracles. I myself have experienced mind-boggling healings with the assistance of etheric physicians and Divine medical teams.

For example, Tanya was a woman in her early twenties who'd injured her back in a car accident. She came to me for a reading, but also asked if I would provide a healing. First, I established that she was getting medical care—she said she was seeing a chiropractor, and also receiving regular physical therapy. I'm a big believer in using all the resources we have available for healing, traditional medicine included.

As I began, I saw that her back had opened energetically along the spinal cord, and this area was filled with circuitry, lights, and wires—the kind of thing you'd see if you imagined a computer chip, but massively sized. The moment her back was "opened," a Divine medical team arrived at my right side. This was a group of five to eight small beings, shorter than me, who presented as a team or a unit that worked together. They did not look human or alien; they didn't look like angels or guides either. They were something different.

At first, they directed me to use my hands to work on the circuits, but I couldn't understand what to do. I stepped aside, and they went to work with precision and focus. There was no blood, no bone, nothing human about it—it all presented as brightly colored lights and circuitry. I held my hands lightly over Tanya's back while all this was going on, and occasionally touched specific areas as I was directed to do so. Tanya did not feel or see the medical team's presence, but she felt a "buzzing" in her back, and her back felt "tingly," she said. When the session was complete, she reported that her pain was relieved; later still she emailed to tell me that her back had dramatically improved. I encouraged her to continue with her chiropractor and physical therapist, which she did.

Another woman, Grace, asked me to heal her breast cancer; the cancer had been caught early, and she'd already begun a course of medical treatment that was expected to work beautifully. Interestingly, as I sat with Grace and began to intuitively scan her body, I found nothing that looked or felt like cancer or any other disease—no illness presented! However, it became clear to me that Grace was exhausted—she'd been "burning the candle at both ends." I saw a vision of this, and perceived the stress that Grace was under. It was stress, not cancer, that was the problem. The cancer was already cured.

"You've already been healed by the treatments," I told her. "It's worked already."

"That's great," she said, in an uncertain tone.

"How much time do you need to be sick?" I asked her suddenly, flashing on the problem.

"At least till January!" she said, marveling at the truth that came out of her mouth.

Grace's body, in its wisdom, had created an illness so she could slow down. Even though the cancer treatment had already done its work, she still needed the time to recover, and most importantly, to relax. Grace took the next three months off, and after some discussion with her doctors, agreed to finish her treatment. During that time she learned how to live in a new, more relaxed way.

In this case, healing had already happened by the time I was asked to help; however, by helping Grace to understand what her soul really needed, she was able to fully heal both body and spirit.

There are many who believe in miracle healings from the spirit world, and I do, too. However, I also understand keenly that we are earth bodies—and, in many cases, earthly treatment, such as traditional and alternative medicine, is a crucial part of the healing package. If you discover significant diseases in someone you are working on, by all means ask your spirit team to help—but then *also* advise the person to go to their physician or medical practitioner, even if just to confirm they are healed!

I expect that as more of us work in this fascinating realm of Divine healing, there will be even more experiences of healing teams assisting from the other realms. At this point, the ones I have worked with (and there have been dozens by now) have been smaller clusters of beings— short and nondescript, only about four or five feet tall.

Some people have suggested they are a type of alien known as the Greys, but I don't think so. These are most definitely spirit guides, not aliens. There's nothing alien about their energy to me. Don't get me wrong—I'm sure there are aliens out there, alive and well and probably peeking in your window right this minute! But that's not who I sense these "teams" are. They vibrate the same as angels, saints, and Holy Ones.

In the channeled writing I receive, these healing or medical teams are mentioned as a method in which the Divine can work faster and more efficiently, and be more useful. It's sort of a "help us come in and then get out of our way," for now. As far as I'm concerned, anything that facilitates healing is beneficial; I am happy to be a conduit for this type of work.

Healing through heart's opening

So much of what we deal with in this lifetime involves the opening of the human heart. We are Divine beings, souls in bodies, and we are here for soul growth. Yet in the process of soul growth, changes take place in the chambers of the human heart. Not the physical heart, but the emotional heart.

In the channeled writing I received in my first book, *Writing the Divine*, one of the most important teachings or lessons is devoted to the way in which our human heart must open consecutively into the feelings of:

- Pain
- Compassion
- Connection
- Love

Such is the progression of the human heart: from emotional hurts and wounds, to compassion for others and ourselves, to the understanding that we are all connected as One/All/Universe/God, and to the deep flowing of love for ourselves and for others. When we experience this progression from pain to love, we finally understand that love emanates not only from us but also through us—we experience love, we are love, and this extends to not only heal us, but to heal all to whom we are connected as well. Everyone, everything, transdimensionally throughout all time and space.

As you work in healing others, or as you heal yourself, remember that in many cases, the most important thing that needs to be healed is not the injury, or the illness. In almost every situation, the most important thing that needs to be healed is the human heart.

As you have learned already from your journey along the intuitive path, whenever we work in psychic seeing, in psychic hearing, with spirit guides or the departed, or in any of the ways in which we sense energy and move in layers and levels, the information that we receive most clearly is emotional.

The visions we see, the message we receive, the journeys we take beyond time and space—all of these profound experiences affect our emotions, and touch and open our hearts. As you work with others in healing, remember that healing is only partly physical. Again, the opening of the heart into the progressive stages of pain, compassion, connection, and love is profound—this is how our heart opens, and this is the way in which our soul grows.

We are not always able to move through all our stages of heart's opening in one lifetime; some of us may only know pain in a particular lifetime. Some may move to compassion, and go no further. Some many experience complete connection to another as One/All/Divine. And some, those fortunate ones, will progress into the bliss and ultimate heart opening of pure love.

This, of course, is the greatest healing force of all.

Exercise: Heart's Healing

1. Do your setup.

2. Imagine that you are floating upward to the ceiling or sky, and then notice that there's a small doorway in that ceiling or sky. Float through it.

3. Notice that on the other side, a spirit guide is waiting for you who is ready to provide you with healing and heart's opening.

4. Allow the spirit guide to open the skin over your heart; you may wish to place your own hand on your heart as you do this.

5. Notice that your human heart is enclosed in a tin box. You can see the heart inside, but it is fully enclosed in the box. Allow your spirit guide to open this box for you.

6. If you are ready, ask your spirit guide to remove this box from around your heart, and when the box is fully removed, notice how your heart expands; it is now unconfined and constrained. Throw the box out into the Universe, where it will be removed.

7. At this time, allow yourself to feel fully all things that cause you pain, that have hurt you, the hurt you have caused others. Allow yourself to feel this pain, and then if you are able, allow yourself to feel compassion for yourself, and for others.

8. Notice that your heart has enlarged. You may need to increase the opening in your chest, to make more room. Do this now, with your hands or your mind.

9. Consider the idea that we are all One, all in connection to each other, all made up of the same particulate energy. Understand that separation is a myth. Notice how this feels in your heart. You may feel woozy, blissful, altered, and transformed. You may simply feel a deep and abiding sense of peace.

10. Ask for healing in your heart and in your body, and allow your spirit guides to provide you with the embedded emotional meaning of pure love. This may be presented to you as a balm to put on your heart, or a channel of light, or in any other way. Allow yourself to feel and accept this emotion of pure love completely, totally, without resistance.

11. Stay in this place of bliss and joy for as long as you like.

12. When you are ready to return to this particular reality on this day, in this lifetime, simply count back from ten, and return. Notice that your heart feels more free in your chest; you feel expanded and open. Notice that you have been healed, and you may return to this place of healing at any time.

Divine healing is required for purposes beyond time.
The act of healing the physical body is only temporal;
the act of healing the heart is beyond time.

—The Messages

nineteen

View from the Mountain

Congratulations. You've made it. You've unlocked Universal secrets that are your birthright as a Divine being in human form. And the best news is . . . there's still more.

But for now, take a moment and reflect on where you've been. It's been quite a journey, and you've experienced a tremendous amount of soul growth during this time. For now, take a minute and gaze out upon the vistas before you. Look at the expanse of everything you see, from this new view at the top of the mountain.

Just for a moment, recall who you were when you started this path.

And then, understand who you are now.

Many of you will have had a spiritual awakening, or this awakening will soon be arriving to you.

Many of you will have met your spirit guides, and learned that this direct connection to the Divine is always available to you, in any time or place.

Many of you will have become so infused with the Divine that you feel different from the inside out—and you are seeing these changes

reflected in your life. You may have experienced the healing of relationships, or the letting go of relationships that could not heal. You may
have discovered your life's purpose, your life's work. You may have met
your Beloved.

Many of you now understand how to follow the signs, synchronicities, and strands that the Universe is continually dangling in front
of you. And many of you have learned to sense, hear, see, and, most
importantly, *trust* the Divine guidance that is continually provided to
you.

We are never alone. The Divine is with us and within us in all
moments.

Now, take a deep breath. Open your heart in gratitude for the experiences you've had exploring the intuitive path. And understand that
your journey is not yet over. Your transformation has just begun.

Glossary

Angel: A Holy Being and messenger of God in Christianity and other religions.

Ascended master: A spirit entity that is not recently deceased or an angel; an entity that is an ascended spirit guide.

Astral projection: Ability to project one's consciousness to another place, time, or realm while the body remains in the present reality.

Aura blending: The experiencing of merging energy fields with another.

Awakening: The change in consciousness that takes place with psychic or spiritual opening.

Bliss: An ecstatic state of transcendence.

Buddha: The ancient spiritual teacher and Holy One, Gautama Buddha.

Chakra: Term derived from the Sanskrit word meaning "wheel," corresponding to seven energy centers in the body.

Channeled writing: Written messages received from another entity, through trance.

Channeling: The act of receiving information from another entity, through trance.

Clairaudience: The art of psychic hearing.

Clairsentience: The art of psychic feeling.

Clairvoyance: The art of psychic seeing.

Clues: Synchronicities and strands of intuitive information.

Dark energy: Lower-vibration energies such as found in the occult.

Deep knowing: The clear, instantaneous understanding of intuitive information.

Departed: Those who have passed away and transitioned from this life.

Direct connection: The concept of being able to make a direct, two-way connection with the Divine, without a third party or additional process.

Divine: God, the Now, Source, Presence, all names for the cosmic One.

Embedded meaning: The emotional content within intuitive information.

Energy healing: A method of healing in person or from a distance that uses energy as its modality.

Entity: A being, spirit, or presence that is not human.

Family constellations therapy: A method to do relationship healing developed by Bert Hellinger.

Flow: The constant, creative state of the Universe. Also, the act of working with Universal creative energy, Source, Presence, the Divine, the Now, One, God.

Future lives: The lifetimes that are to come.

God: The One, the Now, the Source, Presence, cosmic consciousness, the Universe, the One in which we are all One.

Guru: A holy person, master, or spiritual teacher, especially in Indian and other Eastern traditions.

Heart opening: The path of opening through pain, compassion, connection, and love.

Higher self: The concept of a more evolved spirit self that exists in the subconscious.

Holy Beings/Holy Ones: All entities and beings who are sacred.

Intuitive: Another word for *psychic*.

Jesus: In Christian theology, the Son of God.

Jumping levels: The ability to shift and move effortlessly through different layers and levels of time, space, and more.

Karma: Soul growth over time.

Karmic contract: The agreements we make to learn lessons with souls from past lives, which are played out in future lifetimes until the lessons are complete.

Karmic crossing: The people whose paths we cross, in this lifetime and in past and present lifetimes.

Layers and levels: Other dimensions of time, space, and more.

Left brain: The rational, linear side of the brain.

Lessons: The lessons we learn on our path of soul growth in this lifetime.

Life's path/life's purpose: What we are each put on this earth to do to achieve soul growth.

Light trance: A relaxed state of trance that comes by closing the eyes and deep breathing.

Lock into the hum: The concept of energy vibration of the Universe.

Manifesting: The act of bringing into awareness.

Medical intuition: A method of energetically scanning the body to determine illness.

Meditation: A method of accessing the Divine through breath and stillness.

Medium: A person who receives messages from other realms.

Metaphysics: A branch of philosophy dealing with the cosmic realm.

Mind's eye: The concept of a place in the body in which clairvoyant information is received.

Mystic: A person who practices the spiritual arts.

The Now: The concept of the present time and God as being One and the same.

Past-life regression: A method of experiencing past lives.

Past lives: The lifetimes we lived before this one.

Prayer: A method of petitioning, asking, or speaking to God from your heart; also a religious practice.

Psychic: A person with the innate skill of using intuition as a result of connection with the cosmic consciousness. An intuitive.

Receiving: The act of channeling information and guidance from spiritual entities and Holy Beings.

Right brain: The creative, intuitive, spiritual side of the brain.

Saints: In Catholic and other Christian theology, humans who have become sacred through miracles or works.

Setup: A method of preparing for intuitive meditation or trance.

Shaman: A mystic and/or healer who works in the natural and animal realms, especially in Native traditions.

Soul growth: The purpose of our lives; the concept of spiritual growth as the goal of human life.

Soul-to-soul communication: A method of telepathy between souls.

The Source: Another name for God.

Spirit guide: An entity from the spirit realm who communicates to and through us.

Strands: The clues, signs, and symbols that the Divine uses to move us along our life's path.

Symbiotic healing: The ability of soul mates to heal each other with their presence.

Synchronicity: A seemingly coincidental occurrence of events, as directed by Universal flow.

The 33 Lessons: The channeled writing I received for my first book, *Writing the Divine.*

Trance: A mystic state defined by the ability to connect to and experience cosmic consciousness.

Vibration: A measurement of energy.

Vibrational alignment/vibrational matching: A method of matching energetic vibration.

Vocalized channeling: A method of receiving in which messages are received from another entity through vocalized speech or sound.

Window: The concept of an open portal or place for communication between two or more realms.

Bibliography

Bartlett, Richard. *Matrix Energetics: The Science and Art of Transformation.* Hillsboro, OR: Beyond Words, 2009.

Braden, Gregg. *The Divine Matrix: Bridging Time, Space, Miracles and Belief.* Carlsbad, CA: Hay House, 2007.

Burnham, Sophy. *The Art of Intuition.* New York: Tarcher, 2011.

———. *A Book of Angels.* New York: Ballantine, 2004.

Choquette, Sonia. *Ask Your Guides: Connecting to Your Divine Support System.* Carlsbad, CA: Hay House, 2006.

Cushnir, Raphael. *Setting Your Heart on Fire: Seven Invitations to Liberate Your Life.* New York: Broadway Books, 2003.

Dass, Ram. *Be Here Now, Remember.* San Anselmo, CA: Hanuman Foundation, 1978. Originally published in 1971 by the Lama Foundation.

Day, Laura. *Practical Intuition: How to Harness the Power of Your Instinct and Make it Work for You.* New York: Broadway Books, 1996.

Harvey, Andrew. *The Direct Path.* New York: Broadway Books, 2003.

Hawkins, David R. *Transcending the Levels of Consciousness: The Stairway to Enlightenment.* Sedona, AZ: Veritas, 2006.

Hellinger, Bert. *Farewell: Family Constellations with Descendants of Victims and Perpetrators.* (Translated by Colleen Beaumont.) Heidelberg, Germany: Carl-Auer Verlag, 2003.

Katz, Debra Lynne. *You Are Psychic: The Art of Clairvoyant Reading & Healing.* St. Paul, MN: Llewellyn, 2004.

Livon, Jodi. *The Happy Medium.* Woodbury, MN: Llewellyn, 2009.

Newton, Michael. *Life Between Lives: Hypnotherapy for Spiritual Regression.* St. Paul, MN: Llewellyn, 2004.

Osho. *The Book of Secrets.* New York: St. Martin's Griffin, 1974.

———. *Intuition: Knowing Beyond Logic.* New York: St. Martin's Griffin, 2001.

Pearl, Eric. *The Reconnection: Heal Others, Heal Yourself.* Carlsbad, CA: Hay House, 2001.

Peirce, Penney. *Frequency: The Power of Personal Vibration.* Hillsboro, OR: Beyond Words, 2009.

———. *The Intuitive Way: The Definitive Guide to Increasing Your Awareness.* Hillsboro, OR: Beyond Words, 2009.

Pink, Daniel H. *A Whole New Mind: Why Right-Brainers Will Rule the Future.* New York: Riverhead Books, 2005.

Radhanath, Swami. *The Journey Home: Autobiography of an American Swami.* San Rafael, CA: Mandala, 2008.

Virtue, Doreen. *Divine Guidance.* Los Angeles: Renaissance Books, 1999.

Walsch, Neale Donald. *Conversations with God.* New York: Putnam, 1996.

Wiseman, Sara. *Writing the Divine: How to Use Channeling for Soul Growth & Healing.* Woodbury, MN: Llewellyn, 2009.

———. *Your Psychic Child: How to Raise Intuitive & Spiritually Gifted Kids of All Ages.* Woodbury, MN: Llewellyn, 2010.

Questions

Chapter One Exercise: Entering the Vision

The question that you answered in this exercise is:

What is the relationship or situation that requires my attention most right now? What is the soul lesson I'm being asked to pay attention to surrounding this relationship or situation?

Chapter Eight Exercise: Seeing What Is

The question for the blind reading is:

What is the life lesson I need to pay attention to most right now? What is the best way I can learn it?

To Write to the Author

If you wish to contact the author or would like more information about this book, please write to the author in care of Llewellyn Worldwide Ltd. and we will forward your request. Both the author and the publisher appreciate hearing from you and learning of your enjoyment of this book and how it has helped you. Llewellyn Worldwide Ltd. cannot guarantee that every letter written to the author can be answered, but all will be forwarded. Please write to:

Sara Wiseman
℅ Llewellyn Worldwide
2143 Wooddale Drive
Woodbury, MN 55125-2989

Please enclose a self-addressed stamped envelope for reply,
or $1.00 to cover costs. If outside the USA, enclose
an international postal reply coupon.

Many of Llewellyn's authors have websites with additional information and resources. For more information, please visit our website at http://www.llewellyn.com.

GET MORE AT LLEWELLYN.COM

Visit us online to browse hundreds of our books and decks, plus sign up to receive our e-newsletters and exclusive online offers.

- **Free tarot readings** • **Spell-a-Day** • **Moon phases**
- **Recipes, spells, and tips** • **Blogs** • **Encyclopedia**
- **Author interviews, articles, and upcoming events**

GET SOCIAL WITH LLEWELLYN

Find us on
Facebook
www.Facebook.com/LlewellynBooks

Follow us on
twitter™
www.Twitter.com/Llewellynbooks

GET BOOKS AT LLEWELLYN

LLEWELLYN ORDERING INFORMATION

 Order online: Visit our website at www.llewellyn.com to select your books and place an order on our secure server.

 Order by phone:
- Call toll free within the U.S. at 1-877-NEW-WRLD (1-877-639-9753)
- Call toll free within Canada at 1-866-NEW-WRLD (1-866-639-9753)
- We accept VISA, MasterCard, and American Express

 Order by mail:
Send the full price of your order (MN residents add 6.875% sales tax) in U.S. funds, plus postage and handling to: Llewellyn Worldwide, 2143 Wooddale Drive Woodbury, MN 55125-2989

POSTAGE AND HANDLING:
STANDARD: (U.S. & Canada)
(Please allow 12 business days)
$25.00 and under, add $4.00.
$25.01 and over, FREE SHIPPING.

INTERNATIONAL ORDERS (airmail only):
$16.00 for one book, plus $3.00 for each additional book.

Visit us online for more shipping options.
Prices subject to change.

FREE CATALOG!

To order, call
1-877-
NEW-WRLD
ext. 8236
or visit our
website

How to Use Channeling
for Soul Growth & Healing

Writing
the
Divine

❦

Experience 33 Lessons for Divine Guidance

Sara
Wiseman

"Sassy and approachable, *Writing the Divine* is a great read filled with practical
information on how to listen for the messages from the Divine. But take it
seriously. There is wisdom in this work. *Highly recommended.*"

—Sophy Burnham, author of the *New York Times* bestselling *A Book of Angels*

Writing the Divine
How to Use Channeling for Soul Growth & Healing
SARA WISEMAN

This amazing book shows you that learning channeling and channeled writing isn't just for gurus and psychics—it's as easy as closing your eyes and picking up your pen! In part one, Sara Wiseman shares clear, simple directions for channeling and channeled writing, how to use a journal for spiritual growth, and how to manifest in writing.

Part two invites you to experience directly the transformative power of channeled writing—featuring Wiseman's thirty-three Divine lessons. This inspiring collection of messages received from her spirit guides provides Divine lessons on love, life, and spiritual awakening in this world.

978-0-7387-1581-0, 312 pp., 6 x 9 $16.95

To order, call 1-877-NEW-WRLD
Prices subject to change without notice
Order at Llewellyn.com 24 hours a day, 7 days a week!

YOUR
psychic
CHILD

How to Raise
Intuitive
&
Spiritually
Gifted
Kids
of All Ages

"Hands-down, this book is a responsible and positive approach to what can often be a scary subject for parents and children alike. *Your Psychic Child* might also be called a manual for reaching the Divine."
—**Meg Blackburn Losey, PhD**, author of the internationally best-selling *The Children of Now*

SARA WISEMAN

Your Psychic Child

How to Raise Intuitive & Spiritually
Gifted Kids of All Ages

SARA WISEMAN

Want to take an active role in your child's psychic and spiritual development? This indispensable guide helps parents understand and nurture their uniquely gifted children.

Learn about the psychic awakening process and the talents that emerge with each age, from toddler to teen. Discover how to gently encourage your children to explore and develop their strengths in clairvoyance, energy healing, and mediumship, and teach them how to connect with the Divine. Anchored in down-to-earth parental wisdom and alive with personal anecdotes, *Your Psychic Child* is an essential resource for parents who recognize their child's psychic and spiritual potential.

978-0-7387-2061-6, 312 pp., 6 x 9 $17.95

To order, call 1-877-NEW-WRLD
Prices subject to change without notice
Order at Llewellyn.com 24 hours a day, 7 days a week!